Advance Praise

Motivating Adolescents is an expansive and soulful book that will no doubt offer insight to any parent or educator guiding teens through their most promising – and perilous – years. Drawing on her background as a Waldorf teacher and mother, Robin Theiss invites us on a journey filled with practical wisdom and lessons gleaned from a lifetime of devotion to anthroposophy, science, and mythology. It's a rousing call to the adventure of adolescence.

– **Nicholas Ibarra**, Journalist

Concise, intelligent, and open–hearted, *Motivating Adolescents* will lead you towards a more compassionate relationship with your child, finding/generating the time and space in which their life's purpose may flourish. Robin Theiss is an amazing mentor and coach, bringing deeply nourishing insights into the mysteries of human development in a warm and accessible style. Through the EMERGING process, Robin has condensed her great expertise in adolescent education into both a practical guide and spiritual inspiration for parents. As an educator, I meet many parents who are confused about how best to support their adolescent in negotiating the modern world, who believe that education should be about finding one's purpose in life but can't see that in the available options. Robin is able to explain complex ideas in an accessible way, from scientific research to classical philosophy, woven together with personal stories and analogies which bring the material to life.

– **Campbell Davidson**, Lecturer in Education at Goldsmiths College, University of London and Co–founder of The School of Human Movement

Warm–hearted, practical, and intelligent! Finally an educator provides a thorough understanding of why so many children fall through the cracks. In my thirty-five years of practice, I have witnessed too many of our children failed by our outdated model of education, not the other way around. Robin Theiss combines science, psychology, and direct experience to offer an alternative to traditional education. *Motivating Adolescents* is a comprehensive guide to educate and empower our children.

– **Dr. Alexandra Rosenburg**, Psychotherapist

Intrepid! Who but a highly motivated and intrepid student would even consider taking a teacher training course requiring an airline commute from Orange County to Oakland for thirty weekends a year for three years? Robin's enthusiasm for her commuting adventure inspired three fellow travelers – all of them young employees at the coffee house she owned at that time. In retrospect, I can see how Robin's commitment and determination to pursue the Waldorf teacher training evolved into the program she lays out in this book. Still youthful some twenty years after becoming a flying commuter, she now transmits to her teenage students her sense that the world is waiting to be discovered. Having had to rebound from many of life's challenges, she has succeeded in tempering youthful energy with pedagogical insight. Inspiring others, whether her former employees, her high school students, their parents, or her colleagues and friends, that is her gift. She understands the biographical quagmires facing our youth because she herself is unafraid of the mounting challenge to humanness each of us faces. Her book is a practical guide interspersed throughout with apt, often poignant and revealing personal anecdotes. Robin's humor, and self–effacing yet profound grasp of the issues she presents – qualities I remember well from her time as my student in the teacher training – run through the book and provide us with a hopeful program, a can–do attitude. Let us be intrepid and aspire to grasp it.

> – **Dorit Winter**, Author of several books including,
> *Train a Dog, but Raise the Child: A practical primer*
> and *Fire the Imagination, Write On!*

Motivating Adolescents

MOTIVATING
ADOLESCENTS

Practical Wisdom to Help IGNITE
Your Teen's Inner Drive

ROBIN THEISS

NEW YORK

LONDON • NASHVILLE • MELBOURNE • VANCOUVER

MOTIVATING ADOLESCENTS

Practical Wisdom To Help Ignite Your Teen's Inner Drive

Published in New York, New York, by Morgan James Publishing in partnership with Difference Press. Morgan James is a trademark of Morgan James, LLC.
www.MorganJamesPublishing.com

ISBN 9781631950346 paperback
ISBN 9781631950353 eBook
ISBN 9781631950360 audio
Library of Congress Control Number: 2020933249

Cover Design Concept: Nakita Duncan

Cover Design: Christopher Kirk www.GFSstudio.com

Interior Design: Chris Treccani www.3dogcreative.net

Editor: Emily Tuttle

Book Coaching: The Author Incubator

Author Photo: Danielle Cohen

Morgan James is a proud partner of Habitat for Humanity Peninsula and Greater Williamsburg. Partners in building since 2006.

Get involved today! Visit
MorganJamesPublishing.com/giving-back

For Maya and Sage, my two daughters.
Thank you for continuing to achieve your success with grace,
authenticity, and love. You are the light of my life.

Table of Contents

Chapter 1:
Parenting Is an Adventure

*"The big question is whether you're going to be able
to say a hearty yes to your adventure."*
– Joseph Campbell

Parenting is an adventure of a lifetime. It can be planned, studied, thought about, prepared for, and still, you find yourselves in unknown territory. It is like an adventure to another country. Even though you can read volumes of books about the geography, the laws and customs, the people, the language, and the many experiences others had, nothing quite prepares you for the unexpected realities that meet you when you arrive. The guidebooks, maps, language apps, and all of the recommendations can seem useless when you find yourself lost, unable to find your way, and desperate for anyone to help. As in life, it is in these moments that you have the most opportunity for transformation. Parenting is the ultimate transformational adventure. Once you step on this new soil, with its own language and customs, your life will never be the same.

One of the cornerstones of parenting responsibilities is to provide a good education for your children. You want to provide them with opportunities that will set them up for a successful journey and a happy, fulfilling life. Whether you are in a situation with limited resources, and therefore seemingly limited choices, or you are overwhelmed with the choices you have access to, choosing an education can become a whole journey in itself. Parents are becoming increasingly aware of the need for education to change in order to keep pace with the new developments in the world, especially in the area of technological advancements. They are also learning that education needs to be more than just information acquisition.

Of course, you want your children to be educated and set up for a successful and happy life. However, you also know that part of that success and happiness will depend on their humanness, not just their skills and knowledge. Whether your child becomes a doctor, lawyer, engineer, professor, business owner, or Uber driver, you want them to be good mothers and fathers, kind and loving partners, reliable businesspeople, honest neighbors. and good human beings. You want that not just for your children and yourselves but for the world.

This desire to preserve our children's humanness fuels the need to reevaluate what education means and whether current forms of education are setting up your child for a successful and happy future in a rapidly changing world. The world your children are growing up in is very different from generations of the past. The pressure to present their life not only to their peers but also to the world of social media is increasing rapidly. The line between reality and virtual reality is shifting and becoming more and more elusive. Adolescence is already a challenging journey of self-discovery and connecting with your destiny. Add to that the rapidity of advancing technology, and both your adolescent and you find yourselves in an unknown country without a map or an app and unable to locate your GPS.

Technology and Intelligence

Once your child becomes an adolescent, you may find yourself sitting across the table from an enlarged version of the sweet little child who once snuggled in your lap, brought precious treasures in alms-giving hands, and looked to you for all the answers about the world. But now, you may find yourself sitting opposite the back of a phone with an occasion glance of annoyance at your greeting or question. What happened to your child? Were they abducted and replaced with a scowl-faced version of themselves? The electronic devices are the easy things to blame. They seem to draw the adolescent's attention away from the family, away from real life, and away from being human.

In 2005, American inventor Ray Kurzweil published a book, *The Singularity is Near*, predicting the merging of artificial and human intelligence. One of the barometers of computer capabilities in relation to human intelligence is the Turing test. The Turing test, named after its developer Alan Turing in 1950, is a test measuring a machine's communication ability to see if it can ever become equivalent to or indistinguishable from that of a human's communication. The test would depend on a human judge having a "conversation" with two sources, both hidden from view. One of the "conversationalists" would be another human, the other a computer. A computer or AI (artificial intelligence) passing the Turing Test would be when the human judge cannot distinguish when they are conversing with a human or an AI. Kurzweil predicts this will happen by 2029. (Sitting across from your adolescent, it may seem to be coming sooner!)

How is technology changing our communication with each other? Language and technology are one of the most discussed topics in education today. I remember the initial concern I had not just as an English teacher but also as a parent when cell phones and texting became a popular form of communication. Witnessing the spelling, abbreviations, and sentence structure was horrifying to the educators who dedicated their lives to syntax and diction.

However, we now have research that not only dispels that fear but also highlights the incredible human intelligence of the subsequent generations. Texting and technological communication is not making us dumber; we are using it to further develop our intelligence. Is it possible that the adolescent across from you on their phone is developing their intelligence?

Texting isn't affecting language; it is evolving as its own language. One of the indicators of texting becoming its own language is its development of grammatical nuances, such as empathy markers. Empathy markers occur in every language. They are interruptions in the speech to connect with the listener. In English, we have empathy markers such as "ya know" and "you see," among others. American linguist John McWhorter wrote in a 2005 Time's article:

> The argument that texting is "poor writing" is analogous, then, to one that the Rolling Stones is "bad music" because it doesn't use violas. Texting is developing its own kind of grammar. Take LOL. It doesn't actually mean "laughing out loud" in a literal sense anymore. LOL has evolved into something much subtler and sophisticated and is used even when nothing is remotely amusing. Jocelyn texts "Where have you been?" and Annabelle texts back "LOL at the library studying for two hours." LOL signals basic empathy between texters, easing

tension and creating a sense of equality. Instead of having a literal meaning, it does something – conveying an attitude – just like the -ed ending conveys past tense rather than "meaning" anything. LOL, of all things, is grammar.

One of the most challenging aspects for AI developers is replacing human language. From the example above, it is easy to see why: Human language and communication requires relationship – that is, language requires context. The simple "lol" or a happy face emoji requires the receiver in the conversation to have a particular history and relationship with the sender. For example, if I text a winking face emoji to my daughter, it could mean something very different than if I send it to my partner. Texting requires a higher level of intelligence than standard language because it requires a higher level of context and interpretation; it requires more of our humanity. Therefore, it isn't that the adolescent across from you is developing their intelligence because of the phone in their hands, but *in spite* of the phone in their hands. The human spirit is stronger than these devices. It will continue to rise above, transform, and transcend any threat. However, we must ensure that we are nurturing that human spirit and not allowing it to atrophy.

This continued pursuit to develop our intelligence is why, as parents, you instinctually realize how important it is for your adolescent to continue to have human experiences and how important it is for education to be about cultivating their humanness and their human relationships with one another. The Turing test, mentioned above, will be judged by a human. Therefore, the test will partly be a test of the development of AI, but it will also be about the human judge and their ability to tell the difference. It is more and more imperative to provide your adolescent with human experiences.

Parents have more choices now in choosing an education. There are many alternative private schools, charter schools, and independent study options. In choosing the best education for your adolescent, how do you discern what will best prepare them for success? How do you choose the education that will motivate your adolescent and help them realize their full potential? If education continues down the path of standardization and external measures for assessment, schools will continue to develop curricula that an AI could compute better, creating a generation that could be replaced by better preforming, better computing, and more efficient non-human intelligence. However, if you choose an education that focuses on developing our human capacities to think, discern, judge, conceptualize, empathize, act, and love, then you will be setting up your adolescent for success.

Current State of Education

As my own two daughters were approaching adolescence, I became increasingly aware of the question: Is our current education system preparing our adolescents for success? According to the U.S Department of Education website, "United States has one of the highest high school dropout rates in the world." Why are students becoming more and more disengaged with school?

Even if we turn our attention to those who do seem to engage enough to achieve the "success marker" of getting into a good college or university, we find the same statistics. In a 2008 Forbes magazine article, *The College Dropout Problem*, Federick Hess writes:

> America has a college dropout problem. For all the talk of college costs and whether students can even afford to go to college, we've tended to skip past an equally crucial question–whether students who make it to campus are graduating with a useful credential. The sad reality is that far too many students invest scarce time and money pursuing a degree they never finish, frequently winding up worse off than if they'd never set foot on campus in the first place.

More than half of those students, who worked so hard to prepare, apply, and get admitted to a four-year college, are dropping out. This discussion can even extend to the workplace, where many companies are finding that college graduates are ill-prepared in areas such as socio-emotional intelligence, ethical decision making, and collaborative working or teamwork.

The truth is that most of our education is outdated. We have a 200-year-old factory model education left over from the Industrial Revolution, a model where human capacities are reduced to material standards and measurable commodities. Students are evaluated on GPAs and test scores, and majors in college are often based on earning potential rather than interest. However, with the industrial style of education as our prevailing choice, what do you do to help prepare your adolescent for a successful future? How do you honor the time in which they are living, with the plethora of devices and distractions, and yet preserve their essential humanity? There is a way. Follow me.

This book will take you on an eight-part journey called the EMERGING process. It is a journey that I myself was on as parent. It is a journey that I took many adolescents and their parents on. It is a journey of adventure that requires your courage and commitment in a resounding and lively, "Yes!" This yes will not only help you prepare your adolescent for the future, but it will also allow you to see their true potential and authentic individuality EMERGE and set them up for success!

Chapter 2:
The Journey of Adolescence

*"We must be willing to get rid of the life we've
planned, so as to have the life that is waiting for us."*
– Joseph Campbell

The Hero's Journey of Adolescence

As parenting is an adventure, so too is the journey of adolescence; it is the journey of the adolescent becoming the hero of their own story. When you are struggling to understand your adolescent, try to remember the struggles you yourself had during that time. This time in life is when you are trying to form your identities, find your place in the world, and mask the fact that you feel lost. Just as parenting can feel like the part of the adventure when you are lost and hopeless, so too is the adolescent inwardly feeling lost and hopeless. In order for both you and your adolescent to find your way out, you must have the courage to step into the adventure. The only way out is through!

Joseph Campbell referred to this as the "hero's journey." He was sought out by writers, such as George Lucas, to help write the narration of a classic hero's tale like we discover in Star Wars. These stories and movies appeal to you not just as parents but as a hero of your own life. In his book, The Hero with a Thousand Faces, Campbell discusses his theory of the archetype of the hero: the monomyth, an adventure of the individual who leaves what is familiar and comfortable to seek the unknown and returns transformed in service to their community. Campbell outlines stages of the monomyth, which can be summarized in three parts: the departure, the initiation, and the return.

In the departure stage, the hero lives in the ordinary world but is called out of this world of comfort to the unknown. This is the time in the adolescent's life when they are separating from what they knew and was comfortable and answering a higher calling toward their destiny. Campbell explains that, although the hero is reluctant to follow the calling, there is a feeling of compulsion to answer it, a feeling that ignoring the choice is impossible. During this stage of adolescence, the adolescent may even revert back to childish behavior in an effort to cling to what is known and comfortable. However, it is inevitable that the departure must happen.

The initiation stage begins when the hero crosses the threshold to the unknown or other world, where they face challenges and must learn to overcome them through inner wisdom and self-reliance. The hero eventually reaches "the innermost cave," or the central crisis of their adventure, where they must undergo "the ordeal," where they overcome the main obstacle and undergo "apotheosis" (divine wisdom). Adolescents are standing at a crossing point of a lemniscate, between their known past and their unknown future. Your adolescent's emergence into adulthood will be as triumphant as the hero surviving the ultimate challenge if they can overcome their superficial self and transform into an authentic individual who is able to impart meaning and direction in their life. The hero, and the adolescent, must return to the ordinary world with their wisdom. In the return stage, the heroic adolescent is transformed by the adventure and gains wisdom to share with others and prepared to meet the adult world with insight, wisdom, and direction.

This monomyth can be found not only throughout literature, theater, and film, but also as the story of each of our lives. All of us have a hero's journey; it is the biographical purpose to our life, the connection to our destiny. Working with adolescents is my life's work. Looking back, I can see that so many of the small decisions I made were guided by an intelligent divine wisdom. How I came to work with adolescents can be characterized by three pivotal moments that follow Campbell's three stages of the hero's journey: my departure, initiation, and return.

The Departure

The first pivotal moment in my hero's journey happened when I, myself, was an adolescent. I was fifteen years old and in tenth grade. I had been on a fast track of academics since I was labeled an MGM (Mentally Gifted Minor) at age seven. In grammar school, this came with special privileges of small classes and more individualized attention. I never felt particularly smart; in fact, I felt very ordinary. This feeling of ordinariness was facilitated by growing up in a Lutheran home, where we were always doused with a baptism of humility to snuff out any embers of pride trying to ignite.

However, as I got older, the internal pressure to perform increased. In seventh grade, I received the top score on a standardized test, placing my school in the highest rank. I received an award in front of my whole school. I remember being on stage and feeling, "This is not me. I am not the person they think I am. What happens if they all find out I'm not really that smart?"

Fast forward past years of perpetual panic to high school when I constantly feared I would be discovered for not being who everyone thought I was. I was in tenth grade and sitting in a calculus exam (three years ahead of my peers). As I was looking at the numbers and problems, the page went blank.

All of a sudden, nothing made sense. It was as if everything I knew vanished from my head. I began to panic: "What if I don't do well on this exam? What will happen to my grade? What will the teacher think of me? My parents? My peers?" I was the star student, the model child, the one everyone could rely on. Without thinking, I calmly put my pencil down, took my purse, and left the classroom. Looking back, I think I thought I was going to the bathroom, but then I walked past the bathroom and out of the hall into the corridor, then out of the corridor to the street, then down the street until I finally came to a bus stop. I remember just sitting there. I had no plan. Everything in my life was always planned. *This was not planned!*

I got on the first bus that came. I still have a vivid memory of staring out the window as we drove down Pacific Coast Highway. I had no thought of what I was doing or where I was going. I stayed on the bus until the bus driver said, "This is the last stop. You will need to exit the bus." I got off and found myself in Long Beach, California. I spent the day walking around until evening. Looking back, I think I was in some state of shock or overwhelm. I couldn't call my parents because I knew the sound of their voice would pull me back home. I realized I ran away, but I didn't know what from.

I had a loving and wonderful home. My parents were encouraging and devoted. They never put pressure on me to succeed and only supported my accomplishments. We lived in small town in a small three-bedroom apartment that was walking distance to our local Lutheran church, which we attended every Sunday.

Growing up in the 1970s and 1980s, I was part of Generation X, the generation who ran the neighborhood, had no cell phones and barely any homework, and only the streetlights to call us home. My parents both worked, so I walked to school beginning in first grade with my friends and no adults. At the end of the school day, with my house key on a string around my neck, I would walk home, let myself in, call my mom to say I was home, and go play with my friends or wait for my two older sisters to come home with the daily high school gossip. Dinner was always at 6:00 PM. I had an idyllic life: loving family, good friends, supportive church community, and good grades. I had no legitimate reason to run away from home. My self-absorbed fifteen-year-old self had no idea how much worry I put my parents through.

As the sun began to set and everything was closing, I checked my wallet. I saw that I had thirty dollars left from babysitting. I ended up in a twenty-four-hour donut shop. As I was eating a donut and milk for dinner, a young couple, not much older than I, came in. We talked for a while, and I made up some story about getting kicked out of my house and not having a place to stay. They offered their couch for the night.

During the conversation, they mentioned going to Catalina Island recently. The next morning, I decided, I was going to Catalina. I used the last of my money to purchase a ferry ticket to Catalina. When I arrived, I had no money left and no return ticket home. I just walked around the island for hours, thinking about my life and being overcome by a sense of not belonging to it. Thoughts came of my life ending; not serious suicidal thoughts, but more wonderings of what it would be like to just not have this life anymore, one defined by accomplishments and accolades, heading to a destination I didn't want to go. I had this overwhelming feeling that my life was empty and without meaning – pointless.

I was fifteen years old and alone with no money, no place to stay, and no return ticket to get back home. I found a small cove on the side of a rock cliff and spent the night there. That night changed my life. I realized that my life belonged to me. I had to own my past and I had to create my future. There was no returning to the world I came from. And once I did return, I was no longer the girl who left. I evaluated my relationships, time, and truth differently.

The Initiation

The important thing to remember in the departure stage is that it is only the beginning of the transformation. I was fortunate to have parents who allowed me to step in this transformation, who entrusted me with my own future.

In many ways, the transformation continued throughout my life. I wish I could tell you that, once your adolescent passes through into adulthood, their struggles will be over. However, just as in the hero's journey, the departure leads them to the challenges they will face to undergo the transformation.

This leads me to the second pivotal moment on my hero's journey seven years later. I was twenty-two years old and finishing my senior thesis for university. I was majoring in philosophy and cross-cultural religion, not exactly a major that sets one up for success in the job market. However, I heard that, statistically, philosophy majors scored highest on the LSAT exam (the entrance exam for law school). So, I figured I could redeem my radical choice in major by transforming it into a law degree and having a prestigious and well-paying profession.

Part of the research for my senior thesis was to visit and interview people from different faith communities. One of these communities was a Quaker meeting, which met every Sunday in the basement of a church in downtown Riverside, California. I became very involved with this community, participating in their soup kitchen for the homeless every week and driving down to have peace talks at the Mexican/Californian border. Even after my research was completed, I continued to attend their meetings. It was the one hour each week that I felt at peace. My college days were filled with so much studying and thinking; this time each Sunday just allowed me to breathe. I was just about to graduate, and I was set up to attend law school, until one Sunday.

It was a typical Quaker meeting for worship: the members sat in a circle in silence, waiting for the "movement of the spirit," an inner feeling of being called to share something with the community. I had a feeling of restlessness, not just this morning in the silence, but constantly. My decision to go to law school became increasingly heavy on my soul over the past few weeks. One of the members of the meeting stood during the silence and spoke directly to my hesitations and doubts. He said something along the lines of choosing the unexpected and the unknown. It felt as if he were speaking directly to me.

After the meeting, he approached me and said, "I think this may be for you." It was a postcard-sized appeal to fellow Quakers. Pendle Hill, a Quaker community in Pennsylvania, was looking for two student interns. I had one week to apply.

It was almost like the day I walked out of the math test and ended up in Catalina – I applied (without really knowing why), was accepted, and found myself two months later living in a Quaker community. This year changed my life. Even when we are on the other side of adolescence, opportunities for transformation continue to appear. However, what I learned in this stage was that my experience in adolescence prepared me to accept the challenges presenting themselves to me.

Rather than run away from what was unknown and difficult, I embraced the opportunity to meet my challenges with courage and perseverance. As a parent, I know you don't want to stunt your adolescent's growth by protecting them from obstacles and challenges, but you want to know that they are equipped to grapple with the challenges and that they are confident in their decisions and courageous in accepting the responsibility that comes with them.

This year at Pendle Hill characterizes the initiation stage of the journey because it was during this time that I had to face my biggest challenges and inner demons. I had to turn inward and learn self-reliance and fortitude, as well as the value of silence and listening to the spiritual world. I was able to do this because of the preparation I had during adolescence. People often refer to Generation X as the "abandoned generation" or "latch key kids." It's true, I did wear my house key around my neck, but I also grew up much more self-reliant, and that prepared me for an adolescence that was much more independent from my parents than my own children were from me. In generations past, we carried more responsibility for our failures. As an adolescent, I knew that the I was accountable to my journey, to my destiny, that I was the creator of my life. I was the hero of my own story. We need to bring this self-reliance back to our youth and entrust them to find their way through a journey of failures and mistakes.

The Return

The third pivotal moment in my hero's journey was thirteen years later. I was thirty-five years old and enrolled in a Waldorf teacher training program. The director of the program and my mentor, Dorit Winter, suggested that I have a conversation with a Christian community priest. I was at a crossroads in my life and unsure which path to choose.

After finishing my internship at Pendle Hill, I went to graduate school and was given the opportunity to buy a local coffeehouse. I owned and operated the business for over twelve years. It was clear that I could no longer continue with this business and embark on a teaching career. I loved my work with the coffee house, which became a community oasis. We offered poetry evenings, music, open mic nights, and political lectures and discussions. The employees were like a family to me and I couldn't imagine leaving this behind. At the same time, I felt a stronger and stronger pull toward teaching adolescents.

Dorit arranged a conversation with a Christian Community priest. After hearing me speak to my dilemma of which direction to choose, I will never forget the words he said to me: "Your life doesn't belong to you; it belongs to the spiritual world." These words were not spoken out of a view of determinism or fatalism, but rather lifted me out of my own needs and gave me the perspective to see my life in service. His words changed my life and marked the return of the hero's journey. I sold the coffee house and became a Waldorf teacher. I was returning to the world of adolescents, but now with a deeper, more profound sense of destiny, time, and truth.

This hero's journey, of course, continues and had many mini journeys in between. For the last twenty years, I journeyed through the land of teaching early childhood and primary school, but mostly taught in high school. I also embarked on the journey of teaching teachers as an adjunct in teacher training programs around the world. This journey led to a parallel journey of becoming an international speaker at teaching conferences. However, the focus of this book and this part of the journey is guiding adolescents through their hero's journey. For the last ten years, I have been developing retreats and workshops designed to break down the walls of education and redefine success. Once the adolescent realizes they are the hero of their own adventure, the journey can begin; their internal motivation will engage, and things will begin to transform. I consider this awakening of the youth to be my life's work – it is what my own adolescence prepared me for, my early adulthood challenged me with, and my adult life guides me toward. My hope is that working with me helps adolescents and adults go on their own adventure, discover their potential, and return transformed.

Chapter 3:
The EMERGING Process

*"A hero ventures forth from the world of common day
into a region of supernatural wonder: fabulous forces
are there encountered and a decisive victory is won: the
hero comes back from this mysterious adventure with the
power to bestow boons on his fellow man."*

– Joseph Campbell

O n one of my most memorable retreat experiences, I took a group of eleventh graders on a week-long backpacking trip through the Ventana Wilderness in Northern California. It is about a two-day hike into the famous Sykes Hot Springs, where we camped for two days and then hiked out. The hike is lined with coastal redwoods and opens occasionally to meadows of grass. The elevation ranges from 600 feet to almost 6,000 feet, creating steep-sided ridges and deep valleys. This typography of steep mountains and deep valleys gives the wilderness its name: Ventana (the Spanish word for window.)

With amazing views of the ocean peaking though the V-shaped window of the mountains, the contrasting elevation creates many climbs, followed by descents, and then more climbs. Under normal circumstances, this would be challenging enough, but add a fifty-pound pack, a group of adolescents, and the responsibility for their lives, and the backpacking trip takes on a whole new level of difficulty.

Of course, the adolescents were eager at first, almost racing to the first peak. Their chatter was filled with enthusiasm and excitement about their lives and the anticipation of the hot springs ahead. Then, after a few steep, almost stair-like climbs, their enthusiasm waned. Soon enough, the complaints began about the futility of descending only to climb. The backpacks began to weigh more, and our legs began to fatigue.

The sure-footedness they began the trail with soon became reduced to a very shaky, careful placement of each step on steep rocky mountain sides. The chatting began to quiet and there were long silences only interrupted by sounds of a nearby rushing river, a bird, or the labored breathing of the person closest to you.

We stopped where we could find shade, hydrated, snacked on a handful of trail mix or granola bar, and kept moving. When hiking that type of elevation with a fifty-pound pack, you realize the benefit of continuous motion.

Although we were tempted to repeatedly stop and shed our packs to rest, the effort to get back up and hoist the backpack back on to a balanced position was more exhausting than to slowly keep moving.

There was one student whose legs began to become very weak, and the others offered to take on some of his pack. The camaraderie of a shared difficult journey was best expressed in the moment we reached a peak and discovered a rare grouping of Santa Lucia Firs, spire-like trees only found in these mountains. They looked out of place and distinguished among the redwoods; they looked daring and different; they looked endangered and yet courageous; they looked like us.

My colleague, who was a botanist, explained how their root system is wide-spreading and lateral as well as downward. It reaches out to connect to the root system of other trees, enabling it to grow its own roots deeper. A day into the trip, helping and encouraging each other over peaks and across steep terrain, sharing simple meals, and resting under the stars together gave us a sense of this root system of the trees. We can know ourselves more when we share ourselves and our resources with others.

The second day into the trip, we were walking along with the sound of a rushing river, which about mid-day became not just a sound but an obstacle we had to cross. We had two choices: cross over a fallen tree about ten feet above the rushing river or cross the chest high river with backpacks held overhead.

With the possibility of staying dry, most of them chose the fallen tree. I chose the river. First, I wasn't confident in balancing the pack and walking on a moss-covered tree trunk; and second, I thought, if someone falls in, I'll need to go in after them anyway. Watching them cross above me was amazing. Some chose to walk steadily, others dropped to their knees and crawled, and then there was one who chose the "seated scoot." This was so curious to watch because once she had committed to the scoot, she had no choice but to go forward....one inch at a time. Whether above, across the fallen tree, or below, refreshed but wet, we all made it across with focus, determination, and tremendous courage.

By the end of day two, we made it to the hot springs. Here we would camp and rest for two days until we packed up and headed back out. The springs and creeks were absolutely magical. The hot spring emerges from geothermally heated ground water rising from the earth's crust. It is about 102 degrees Fahrenheit. We sat in these pools and had the most fascinating conversations, mostly characterized by wondering how the hot springs came to be, which led to questions about the indigenous cultures and the nature surrounding us. My colleague and I did our best at providing answers, but most of the education remained in the state of inquiry and wonder. Questions, no doubt, the student carry with them today, as do I.

There was one student who was visiting from Beijing, China. He grew up the city his entire life and never went camping or spent a night in nature. On one of our rest days, I saw him sitting on a log watching the leaves fall from a tree for hours. He later shared with the group that it was the most amazing and thought-provoking experience he ever had. He described an epiphany he had about the falling leaves and their sense of timing and purpose, that they had their time and were now releasing their life over to another form of life. There isn't a textbook in the world that could have taught him as extensively.

After two nights, we packed up to begin our journey out. The good news was our packs were lighter and our hearts were fuller. The climb up and down the mountains and valleys seemed different than our journey in. We were filled with a tremendous sense of gratitude for our own courage to face the many challenges, gratitude for each other, and gratitude for this incredible wilderness of *ventanas* – windows to the world and paths to our souls.

The EMERGING Process

The EMERGING process is much like this backpacking trip: it begins with a shaking up of the ground beneath our feet, requiring mindfulness and empathy toward others. When faced with challenges, we must be willing to take risks and have courage. This is grit. Eventually, we will arrive at new relationship with the world and ourselves, one of inquiry, facilitated by a study of nature and finally arrive with a true appreciation for life in a new way- gratitude. This book will be a journey through the EMERGING process –

*E*ducation

*M*indfulness

*E*mpathy

*R*isk

*G*rit

*I*nquiry

*N*ature

*G*ratitude

Education

This first step of the process is a shaking up of our ideas of success and education. Just as the back packers began the journey confident, vibrant, and ready to reach our destination, when you first became a parent, you imagined your child's future with enthusiasm and hope. This confidence begins to wane as the pack of expectations, pressure to succeed, and ideas of success and education don't seem to be working for your child. Using Plato's analogy of the cave to understand the shadows of education, the chapter will begin to question the purpose of education and shift your focus from purely academic accomplishments to looking at education from a soul development perspective. Drawing on twenty years as a Waldorf teacher and student of anthroposophy, I will provide a different way of seeing education as a process of connecting with one's destiny and path in life, rather than adhering to an Industrial Revolution style of educational conformity.

Mindfulness

Reframing old paradigms requires mindfulness. Just as the backpackers had to quiet their conversations and begin to pay attention to their foot placement and breath, so too must the adolescent quiet the chatter of the world and begin to go inward. Turning inward is the first step in self-reliance. It is the beginning of developing their confidence in their inner voice. In this chapter, I will share with you my experience at Pendle Hill, a Quaker Community for Study and Contemplation, where I met and studied with a Buddhist priest. It was through this cultivation of mindfulness that I was able to understand Martin Heidegger's concept of non-linear time, a concept that is supported by writers and thinkers such as Abraham Hicks and Dr. Joe Dispenza. Cultivating a practice of mindfulness brings a new perspective of time- a quantum perspective, bringing the future to the present moment.

Empathy

At the pinnacle of our long climb, the experience of the finding the grouping of Santa Lucia Firs, the trees whose roots form horizontally and then deepen, will stay with me forever. This gesture of empathy, the capacity to support yet stay an individual, is the next part of the EMERGING process. In this chapter, I will share some of the corresponding brain research associated with empathy and how cultivating this capacity helps awaken your adolescent to their own sense of self. The chapter will continue to explore the different types of relationships in your adolescents' life: their relationships with parents and family, relationships with teachers and mentors, and relationships with peers. The last part of the chapter will explore C.S. Lewis' *Four Loves* and how they relate to empathy and adolescent development.

Risk

When we first encountered the river we had to cross, there was a moment I thought we should turn around and go back. But, after assessing the depth of the water and the sturdiness of the fallen tree, I knew it was possible. It was risky, but not impossible. Adolescents will also encounter obstacles in their path. Learning to differentiate between recklessness and risk is important. Had the tree not been sturdy or the river more dangerous, crossing would have been reckless. Risk taking is part of a normal, healthy adolescence. In this chapter, I will share research about adolescent brain development and risk taking. I will also share examples of how risk taking is important for connecting with a higher purpose and destiny. It allows us to lift ourselves out of our own needs and connect with a greater sense of belonging to the world and to each other.

Grit

The partner to courage and risk taking is grit, the capacity to see something through. The one student who chose to sit and scoot her way across the log had to stay committed to her choice. It took a very long time and probably more effort and more sustained courage than any of the other choices. She had to face the ten-foot drop with the rushing river below each inch of the scoot. However, she had no choice, really; once she committed to that way of crossing, there was no turning back. Getting up on her hands and knees and crawling or, even more dangerous, trying to stand balancing a heavy pack would have landed her in the river for sure. How did she get across?

Determination and pure grit. This capacity to endure our choices is essential in adolescent development. In this chapter, I will use the story of Siddhartha to frame the discussion of grit. Exploring Rudolf Steiner's understanding of reverence, we can begin to see how our will forces and our capacity to love can help strengthen our resolve and determination. Through our capacity to follow through with our commitments and develop "stick-to-it-ness," we become people of integrity.

Inquiry

Once we arrived at the hot springs and were able to settle, we became filled with wonder and awe. The world became a catalyst of inquiry and curiosity. In this chapter, I will begin with the story of Valentin Achek Deng, one of the Sudanese Lost Boys. His autobiography recounts the story of his childhood which gives the book its title, *What is the What*. His life-long search for this answer becomes a model of searching fueled by human curiosity, disappointment, and, finally, self-realization. Also in this chapter, I will share the importance of using Socratic dialogue in education. This process not only allows each person to enter the conversation without feeling judged or afraid they may have the wrong answer but also encourages the wisdom of each individual to emerge.

Nature

Surrounded by the coastal redwoods, flowing rivers, and natural hot springs, it is no wonder that the student from China had this overwhelming experience of watching the leaves fall. Spending time in nature is an essential part of the EMERGING process. In this chapter, I will share some experiences from our retreats in Idyllwild and some of the poems the students wrote while on this trip, demonstrating the effect immersing oneself in nature can have on our soul.

Gratitude

Hiking out of the Ventana Wilderness, we were filled with an overwhelming sense of gratitude for our courage and abilities, each other, and the nature around us. Gratitude is not only a necessary component to the EMERGING process; it is a natural result. In this chapter, I will share two experiences I had with loved ones at the end of their lives. These experiences of witnessing someone reflect on their life while facing death instilled in me a new sense of time. This type of gratitude and deep love is what I try to bring to the participants of the retreats. I will share one of the exercises we do with the participants to shift their perspective of priorities and deepen our relationships. When we experience this level of profound gratitude and love, not only does time merge into one sacred moment but we also merge into our true selves.

Importance of Retreat

In my twenty years in education, I never witnessed more transformation than when the students step out of their everyday life, unplug from the virtual world of social media, and connect with nature. The retreats allow them to fully participate in the EMERGING process. It is difficult to evaluate and contemplate your life when you are in the day-to-day grind and routine. Usually, the first day of the retreats is the day of decompressing and detaching. It takes the adolescents some time to let go of the reverberation of the demands and habits of life to find stillness. However, once they silence the devices of distraction, the whisper of their inner voices grows louder. These eight stages of the EMERGING process are about cultivating their inner voice, fostering confidence to listen to it, and building courage to act upon it. As a parent, I know you long to see your adolescents engage with their life in a meaningful way. The first step toward this internal motivation is allowing the adolescent to see their life objectively and begin to separate their thoughts about themselves and the world from their feelings about themselves and the world. The retreat gives them the proper space and distance to do this.

EMERGING Role of Parents

The EMERGING process is a journey into the wilderness of one's soul. There will be challenges and obstacles that require inner fortitude and courage; there will be moments of extreme beauty and reverence; there will be moments of confusion and disorientation; there will be moments of recognition and validation to what you have always known in your hearts but never heard someone say out loud. No matter how thick the wilderness of parenting adolescents becomes, your inner light will guide you out of the darkness and you will emerge as well. The EMERGING process is both the adventure of the adolescent and the parent. Now, let's go on a journey together, help your adolescent discover their potential, set them up for success, and EMERGE into their future!

Chapter 4:

Education– An Essential Component for Success

"The privilege of a lifetime is being who you are."
– Joseph Campbell

Understanding the purpose of education is essential to your adolescent's success. However, in order to understand this, you must first become clear about what you mean by success. Three months before the release of *A Streetcar Named Desire*, *The New York Times* published an essay by Tennessee Williams titled *A Streetcar Named Success*. It is brilliant, thought provoking, and haunting.

In this essay, Williams shares his experience of being catapulted to success almost overnight by the popularity of his play *Glass Menagerie*. He writes about moving from his small apartment to a Manhattan hotel suite with room service and maid service on demand. He recalls staring at the green, satin couch and hoping that in the morning the green, which looked like the slime at the bottom of a pond, would grow more beautiful by morning, that these luxuries surrounding him would feel less foreign and more comforting, and that his aversion would turn to acceptance. It didn't. In fact, he abhorred the couch even more in the morning, as he did his success.

Success, he realized, came at the cost: himself. As his diet of room-serviced meals makes him too fat for his old and worn $125 suit, he began to rethink his desire for success. Like *A Streetcar Named Desire*, the streetcar serves as a metaphor for the journey through life – some streetcars are fueled by desire, some by success. I am often asked by parents what type of education will set their child up for success. This can only be answered if we first talk about what success looks like and the purpose of education in the adolescent's journey. Before we hop on the streetcar, we need to know where we are going and what it will cost to get there.

What Is Education?

One of my favorite analogies of education is in Plato's Republic. In this Socratic dialogue, Plato gives us the analogy of the cave. Plato, through Socrates' presentation, presents a situation in which there are people who were imprisoned their whole lives and bound and chained in such a way that they cannot turn their heads, but can only look forward. They are in a cave, staring at one of the walls and the shadows being cast on the wall. Having been here their whole lives, they know nothing else. The shadows they see on the wall are coming from objects behind them. More specifically, there is a constant fire behind them and between them and the fire is a walkway where people are walking and carrying various objects on their heads. When they pass by the fire, the walkway dips down so only the shadow from the object on their head is cast.

For example, let's say someone is carrying a bowl on their head. When they pass, the light of the fire casts a shadow on the wall the prisoners are observing. The prisoners made a game out of being able to first guess what the object is before the shadow becomes detailed enough to identify the object. At first, the bowl is an amorphous round shadow, and as the light of the fire comes directly behind it, its outline becomes more precise. The prisoners experience this further definition as a process of gaining knowledge of something.

Plato suggests the next scenario of one of the prisoners being freed. As he is unbound and first turns to see behind him, he is blinded by the light of the fire and is afraid. He does not want to be free. In fact, he has to be taken out against his will. Once outside the cave, he sees shadows of objects in the world; for example, a shadow of a tree being cast from the light of the sun. He immediately identifies with the shadow as reality, since this is all he knows. Eventually, he begins to learn that the shadow is representing something, namely the tree itself.

Now, Plato asked us to imagine what will happen when the freed prisoner returns to the cave to tell the others. He suggested that when he returns, his eyes will have a hard time readjusting to the darkness. When he tries to tell the others of his experience, they will not believe him and ask him to prove his knowledge by beating them at the shadow game. With his eyes still adjusting to the darkness, he will not be able to make out the shadow as fast. He will appear dumb, and his experience will be labeled fantasy and delirium.

Education Is Emerging from Darkness to Light

This analogy by Plato serves as a deeper understanding of education. Education comes from the Latin *e-ducere* – "out from" and "to draw;" in other words, "to draw out from." Like Plato's cave analogy, a true education, then, is the leading out from the darkness to the light. However, what is important to note is that this leading out comes from within the person. It is a drawing forth from the individual.

The EMERGING process facilitates this emerging of the individual. Most of our current forms of education are concerned with giving knowledge and instructing. Whereas the root of the word "educate" comes from the gesture of drawing forth, the root of the word comes from the Latin *in- struere* – *in*, "on," and *struere,* "to pile, build" – "to pile on." We built an education system predicated on the idea of piling knowledge on the child rather than drawing forth their inner capacities and wisdom.

This model of "piling up on" education is a product of a 200-year-old education system built to serve the model of the Industrial Revolution. It was designed with the intention to offer a free, accessible education to all. In order to serve the masses, education was set up like an assembly line where everyone moved down the conveyor belt and received information in each grade level, piling up the information, until the managing of this pile becomes assessed by the students' ability to regurgitate what was given. This piling up is done without regard for the inner life of the child and their individual needs. Rather, it assumed that each student needed the exact same information, presented in the same way, in the same amount as those that passed though before.

In Charles Dickens' novel *Hard Times*, he depicts the beginning of this factory style of education. Dickens suggests that the setting in nineteenth-century England and the height of industrialization threatens to turn human beings into machines by suppressing the development of their emotions and imaginations. The opening scene of the novel has the teacher demanding "facts, facts, facts." This regards knowledge as the accumulation of facts that can be repeated, making education measurable and uniform.

In the exchange between the young and free-spirited student Sissy and the teacher Mr. McChoakumchild *(his name says it all!*), we can see how this suppression first began. When Sissy cannot give the scientific definition of a horse, she is assessed as not being able to know one of the most common animals. Dickens depicts the slow conversion of everyone in society becoming servants to the machine. We lose our humanity and our capacity to navigate with our moral compass. Ethics are reduced to relativism where the discernment of the human being is despondent in the face of injustice and inequality. Those iniquities become the responsibility of a system rather than of a human. As Dickens' writes:

> It is known, to the force of a single pound weight, what the engine will do; but not all the calculators of the National debt can tell me the capacity for good or evil, for love or hatred, for patriotism or discontent, for the decomposition of virtue into vice, or the reverse, at any single moment in the soul of one of these quiet servants, with the composed faces and the regulated actions.

Streetcar Going Nowhere

Many of our education models continue this approach, leading to a current generation that is more anxious, depressed, and less prepared for life than ever before. We spent decades of money, resources, time, and energy keeping up with the increasing pace of the conveyor belt, but have not stopped to evaluate where the belt is going. Students are reduced to test scores, GPAs, and statistics, and yet they are not able to navigate their own journey or themselves. Colleges and workplaces continue to comment on the lack of social skills of our youth, failing simple tasks such as getting along with their college roommate, advocating for themselves when against obstacles, or seeking out their professors/mentors when they have questions. Their conveyor belt has become a Williams-style "streetcar going nowhere." They lack the necessary life skills to engage the streetcar toward a destination matched with an inner calling toward their destiny.

Even those who do manage to engage and who are admitted to top universities and land prestigious and well-paying jobs often find themselves forty-years-old, lost in a dead-end job, in the middle of a divorce, or having an identity crisis. Why? Because they lost themselves in the journey of success. They, like Williams, do not recognize their Manhattan suite life, the ones that steal their true identities, the ones that come with green-slime-colored couches and room service. In striving toward the elusive designation of success, they bought into the room-serviced education, the one that fattens us up but makes us too fat for our soul, the one that everyone wants until they have it. It is a success that comes at an exchange not worth the cost, because it is an exchange of their individuality. It is exchanged for a statistic, a chart, an acceptance letter, a promotion, or an award. Success is only success if you recognize yourself once you get there. A true education, one that draws forth inner capacities, sets your adolescent up for this recognition. It is an education that keeps their individuality intact, and their soul as the driver on their journey to success.

Many of the youth I work with now are in their early twenties. They are on the other side of adolescence, and yet they are not able to take hold of their life. Somewhere along the way, they relinquished the steering of their life over to outside expectations. They find themselves mid-way through college, piled in debt without any sense of what comes next, or under constant scrutiny for not having gone the college route and now having to prove their success.

My first task is to establish that their life belongs to them, both the decisions they make in life and the consequences for those decisions. I ask them first to set intentions for themselves – not just goals, but intentions. The difference is that the intention requires their active participation, rather than a goal, which is something they long for or want to happen. An intention binds their actions with the result.

In the beginning of our work together, I have them set intentions each day without a deliberate benefit of the intention in mind. For example, the intention may be to spend time outdoors, or to be on time to every commitment. The benefit of the intention itself – better health or greater respect – is secondary. What is important is that they begin to engage in their life. When they are not able to fulfill an intention, that is also great! That is where the work can begin. Their soul then becomes engaged in bringing them into their future. This engagement is a soul education.

Anthroposophy and Soul Education

I have worked in Waldorf education for the past twenty years. This educational model is based on the writings and indications of Rudolf Steiner and anthroposophy. I will be using that lens to shed light on what I mean by "soul education." Although there are different philosophies that coincide with anthroposophy, I have yet to come across one that is so complete and encompassing on addressing the issue of a soul education. In the analogy of the cave above, Plato likened the soul to the human eye. Just as the human eye is the sense organ of observing the visible world, so is the soul the organ through which we come to know things and have reason.

Anthroposophy can be described in its name, *anthropsophia,* which means "the wisdom of the human being." In this philosophy, wisdom is inherent in the human being, not something that can be given or attained. The task of the teacher is not to teach but to awaken. In his book *Theosophy*, Steiner proposes that we can develop organs of perception to connect with our spiritual being: "Just as in the body, eye and ear develop as organs of perception, as senses for bodily processes, so does a man develop in himself soul and spiritual organs of perception through which the soul and spiritual worlds are opened to him." Developing these organs of perception is the purpose of our incarnation and is the way in which we harmonize our spiritual being within a physical being. This coming together of spirit and body creates a soul, similar to how blue and red together make purple.

In anthroposophy, our soul is dependent on the spiritual and bodily nature coming together. Just as if you took blue or red out of the mix, the purple would disappear, if the body or spirit is not in the mix, the soul also is not there. The eternal part of us, then, is the spirit, and the soul is the vehicle through which we find the harmonizing of this spirit body into our physical body and thus take up our journey.

Recognizing the spiritual component of the human being is essential in education. In more traditional forms of education, this spiritual component is left out in an attempt to protect religious freedom. It is important to acknowledge the spirit does not preclude religious freedom. Rather, it has the possibility of supporting religious freedom. Furthermore, in anthroposophy, this view of the human being as body, soul, and spirit is a way of understanding the developing child. It is not meant to be taught as a doctrine in the curriculum. It informs the curricular approach and supports the inner development of both parents and teachers. Education without the spiritual understanding becomes dry and informational. This content-driven approach is not what is needed for our future. We live in an age where we have access to the information. However, what we need is soul education, one that equips the developing child and adolescent with capacities to impart meaning and purpose to their future.

Human Development: Seven-Year Cycles and the Three-Part Brain

As a parent, you want to provide the very best for your child. You want to know that you did the best you could with the knowledge that you had. Brain development is one of the research areas that is providing information to help us as parents make sound decisions. Understanding how the brain develops throughout your child's life can help you make informed decisions about education. Furthermore, research in brain development suggests that a healthy soul education is also a healthy brain education.

In applying anthroposophy to education, Steiner looked at child development in successive seven-year cycles. The purpose of these seven-year cycles is to harmonize the spirit within the body of the developing person. This harmonizing happens in the soul. Therefore, Waldorf education, which is built on this understanding, is aimed at being a soul education; it is the harmonizing of the spiritual aspects of our nature with our earthly or bodily incarnation. The seven-year cycles correspond to developmental needs and changes within the human being during the periods of life. This view of human development also coincides with current research in brain development and maturation.

During the first of the seven-year cycles, from birth to seven-years old, the child is building up their physical body. This is the time when our physical bodies grow the most. For example, take a look at the physical aspects of our brain and how it grows in mass. At birth, the brain is about twenty-five percent its adult weight. By age two, it is at seventy-five percent its adult weight. It is then at ninety-five percent by age six, and finally at one hundred percent by age seven. This, of course, does not indicate its developed capacities, but from a purely physical point of view, the most development happens during this time span.

In this first cycle, also known as early childhood, we are also developing the stem portion of our brain. The healthy development of this is best supported by the use of our physical body, such as by learning to crawl, stand, walk, play in sand, climb trees, run after our pets, etc. It is also important to note that current research suggests open-ended play for this period of development. In early childhood programs, this translates as playing outside and with natural materials as opposed to early introduction of screens or early literacy programs.

In the second seven-year cycle, from ages seven to fourteen years old, we are developing what is called in anthroposophy our *etheric bodies*, or life bodies; in other words, our life forces. This is the part of us that learns through rhythm and repetition. One way to understand this stage of development is to compare a rock to a plant. A rock has a physical body. A plant also has a physical body, but in addition, it grows and reproduces. This is not to compare the growing child to a rock the first seven years and then a plant the second seven years but rather to understand that the differentiation between the rock and plants. Namely, the life forces are the part of the child that is developing during this stage in development.

The second phase of brain development is the limbic part of the brain, corresponding to the second seven-year cycle when the etheric or life body is developing. This development happens in the primary school years. Our limbic system is best developed through attaching meaning to learning. In Waldorf education, this is paramount. The students are given subjects that move them, that can continue to live and grow in their imagination. Also in Waldorf schools, you will often find multiplication tables being taught using rhythm sticks and other rhythmic means (bean bags, etc.). This rhythmic learning also supports the limbic portion of the brain development.

In the third seven-year cycle, from fourteen to twenty-one years old, the human being develops what is called in anthroposophy the astral body. Another way to think of this is the desire body, or the part of us that is ruled by wants and desires. Continuing the comparison of the rock and plant above, one way to understand the differentiation of the astral body or desire body is to observe an animal. Like a rock, an animal has a physical body, and like a plant, an animal has an etheric or life body; however, unlike a rock or plant, the animal can self-propel. It can move toward its desires. Again, I am not equating the adolescent to an animal; rather, understanding this gesture of moving toward our desires helps us to understand the astral body or the desire body.

This also explains the behavior of adolescents, which is driven by lack of impulse control and the inability to delay gratification. The part of the brain that is developed during this third stage is the neo-frontal cortex. According to the most recent research, this is not completely developed until our early twenties, corresponding to the incarnation of what anthroposophy calls the ego, or the I. The I is the distinguishing attribute of the human being from the rock, the plant, and the animal kingdoms, corresponding to the ability to make decisions based on future results, override impulses and urges, and connect through thinking to the spiritual world.

Adolescent Soul Education and Success

Because I primarily work with adolescents and have the most experience with this third stage of development, I would like to focus now on the nuancing of this stage in order to understand what I mean by a soul education and why it is essential for success. The journey of adolescents or the stage from age fourteen to twenty-one is akin to Plato's cave analogy – it is the leading out of darkness to the light, from images to reality.

In ninth grade, the student usually arrives in high school with the lens of polarity. That is, the student sees the world in extremes: they love something one day, hate it the next; their best friend becomes their worst enemy; their favorite teacher, their worst nightmare. This view of the world is not only healthy but necessary. In a Waldorf high school, the subjects are taught through the polarities: comedy/tragedy, thermodynamics (heat/cold), geometric drawing (center/periphery), etc. The idea is we use their lens, namely polarities, to introduce the subjects, educating not just their mind but their soul as well. The analogy I often give to parents is this: Imagine if we were all standing around a tree. Although we are all looking at the same tree, each of us has a slightly different perspective. The ninth grader, or fourteen-year-old, is deluded in believing that their perspective is *the* perspective rather than *a* perspective. The goal of this stage of soul development is to get the student to move from their perspective and consider other perspectives – to walk around the tree, per se, and see other points of view.

In tenth grade, the next stage of soul development comes by seeing the relationship between those perspectives and polarities; in other words, how one's perspective relates to another and how, together, the perspectives can form a knowledge of the tree. This stage of soul development is synthesis and can be seen in subjects like chemistry (acids/bases), physics (mechanics), history (ancient cultures), and English (history of language). All of these subjects are approached from the point of view: How does one thing relate to another.

Now, the interesting part of this stage of development is the experience the student has of unknowing. It is as if they have successfully walked around the circle and come to see that their perspective was limited and incomplete. They now can see how all of the perspectives add to the picture, but they now have lost their own solid point of view. It is as if the world is constantly morphing and changing and they have nothing to hold on to. The adolescent at this age is often plagued by a feeling of emptiness, a great inner chasm that cannot be named or identified. This is sometimes referred to as the dark night of the soul. Across cultures, this is the highest jump in suicide rates and the most prevalent age of drug and alcohol introduction. This is a crucial time for their soul education. The extent to which the adults around the fifteen- or sixteen-year-old can love them without filling them up with accolades and criticisms, the more we can keep the chasm or emptiness free. Then, the more there will be space of what comes next in the eleventh grade.

The eleven grader or sixteen-/seventeen-year-old then begins to emerge from the dark night, from the cave, from the inferno of their soul; the sun begins to rise. What emerges from that darkness is a true authentic individual – not a copy of a shadow or a fulfillment of someone else's expectation, but a true individual. This individual is now ready to begin the process of true learning – learning in alignment with their destiny. This can be seen in Waldorf subjects like Parzival, a German medieval romance about a journey to discover one's holy grail, or projective geometry, the mathematical concept of infinity. This is the year of analysis and research, the process of deconstructing other points of view and reconstructing your own.

This transformation into individuality prepares the student for twelfth grade and beyond. The twelfth grader, or seventeen-/eighteen-year-old, is poised to meet the world. In subjects like Russian literature, the Transcendentalists, and bio-chemistry, the student begins to see the value of the human being in the world. They begin to engage in a life of serving out of their gifts and capacities. If they had a soul education, they are open minded, socially intelligent, and aware of their own gifts and capacities. They stand with confidence, waiting for their own streetcar, whatever its name. They are able to recognize and name the green satin couches of life. Moreover, having a soul education gives them the courage to return to Plato's cave and try to explain reality to the others. In choosing an education for your adolescent, it is important that you choose one that fosters their soul capacities, one that recognizing them as a spiritual being without indoctrinating them into a specific religion, leaving them free in their thinking and confident in their capacities.

Chapter 5:
Mindfulness – The Creator of Time

"Your sacred space is where you can
find yourself over and over again."
— Joseph Campbell

When I was twenty-two years old, I found myself not at law school, as I intended, but rather living as a student intern at Pendle Hill, a Quaker community for study and contemplation. It was here that I learned the value of quieting my mind, listening to my soul, and valuing silence. The Quakers have a practice of contemplation. One of my favorite sayings of theirs is reversing the common saying, "Don't just sit there, do something" to "Don't just do something, sit there."

I just finished my undergraduate work at university, four years characterized by doing, doing, doing. Even though I chose philosophy and religion as my majors out of a deep interest, much of my work was in my head. For fun, my fellow philosophy majors and I would engage in mental combats with each other and our professors over a beer at the local pub or late-night arguments over the existence of the table. However, this academic sparring was always turned outward and couched in clever semantics; my reality was informed by my outer circumstances and my thoughts about those circumstances. It wasn't until I was at Pendle Hill that I began to know the difference between being thoughtful and being mindful.

Pendle Hill had a perimeter path around the community, a path that many walked on as a meditation. I walked it almost every day in an inward silence, with my ears open to the sounds of nature. Ralph Waldo Emerson wrote about the "obedience of the spirit" that nature abides by. It is the allowing of the spirit to mold us. The word obedience has the root "to listen." The English word "obey" comes from the Old French *obeir,* which in turn comes from the Latin *oboedire,* which means "to give ear." This listening is not a listening of our thoughts, but rather a listening of our heart, which is in rhythm with the natural rhythms of the universe. It is the birds' morning call, the trees' gentle rustle, the brooks' babble; it is the moments in between that are pregnant with silence – a silence that grows so loud and profound that our inner core almost burst wide open. I began to listen, to really listen; it was if I was deaf my whole life.

The Silent Teacher

Pendle Hill has a practice of inviting religious teachers from different faiths to come as residents to the community. My residency happened to coincide with Dai'en Benage, a Buddhist priest from Japan. She was the one who taught me that silence is sacred. I learned to sit in meditation every morning with her, to spend weeks in silence, and to gaze into the eyes of another with unconditional, non-personal love.

Every morning at six, she would lead us in a morning mediation. It would begin and end with a tone from the striking of a triangle. The first few mornings, I was crawling out of my skin. The time between the first tone and the last seemed like an eternity. The one hour was excruciatingly painful. I tried to play tricks on my brain by counting, by singing different songs in my head, and by making a list of what I had to do. My legs were uncomfortable and falling asleep. I was restless. Time became an annoying passive-aggressive friend who wouldn't just say, "*Done!*"

Dai'en first taught me to simply acknowledge my discomforts without judgement. *Oh, my legs are beginning to tingle. My mind is has not settled yet.* Then, she taught me to acknowledge the sensations and allow them to be. *Oh, my legs are tingling, I will allow them to tingle.* The next step was to allow the sensations while I focused my mind. *My legs are tingling; as they tingle, I will focus my mind on the quiet.* This process of gentle acceptance and direction of eventually turned the hour of mediation into a timeless moment. The time from the striking of the tone to begin the hour to the end of the hour seemed to be one breath. It was the experience of Arjuna in the Bhagavad-Gita, when all of time is suspended in his moment of dilemma, when his focus is so intense and directed that time, in a linear way, stands still. This meditation cultivated an opening to listening in a new way. This new capacity for listening changed my daily walking meditations along the path. I began to listen to the silence, and it became my teacher.

In working with adolescents, I came to appreciate their desire to quiet the noise around them. The problem is they don't know how. Providing them with simple techniques of mindfulness helps them create a space of sacredness within them. This practice of mindfulness can be mediation, prayer, chanting, or simply sitting quietly and focusing their thoughts. This mindfulness gives them a ground on which to stand when their world begins to shift and change.

Groundlessness

Pema Chodron, a contemporary American Buddhist, speaks of the experience of groundlessness, or the condition of having the ground beneath us taken away. It is here that we begin our path. Oftentimes, adolescents will create this groundlessness. It may come in the form of failed grades and disengagement in school, bad relationship choices, substance abuse, or rebellion/resistance to family and family traditions. This groundlessness is the first necessary step in finding one's path. Up until this point, the path your child was taking is not their own but rather the path that was provided for them. No matter the comforts you provided, adolescents will create situations of groundlessness. This is necessary, for it is not until they experience this groundlessness that they can turn inward and find their innermost self.

Thus, turning inward is the first step toward mindfulness. At first it is uncomfortable. What I learned studying with Dai'en was that what was crawling out of my skin when I couldn't sit still was like a detox of the pollutants of life. It was all of the things that came to artificially define me. When we take away all of those definitions, we are left with our authentic selves.

I like to do this exercise with adolescents to begin this process. First, make a list of everything you think you are: a soccer player, a student, a son or daughter, a musician, an American, a girl/boy, etc. Now, imagine each description was taken away one at a time. Would you still be who you are? For example, if you could no longer play soccer, and therefore were not a soccer player, would you not be you? Then, I ask them to go through the list and cross out anything that would not take away the essence of who you really are. The lists become shorter and shorter.

Eventually, through some discussion, we can cross everything off the list. At times, some adolescents refuse to let go of some identity markers, like their gender and familial relationships, but even further dialogue would loosen the grip of these. The point I try to get to is this: Who are we without those outside definitions? I am not soccer player. I am not student. I am not daughter/son. There is even something beyond being boy/girl. Who am I? This is often a profound, groundless moment for the adolescent. If I am not all of that, who am I? Now, the real work can begin. We can begin the adventure of discovering this I.

Suspending Time

The first step in this discovery of I is the cultivation of mindfulness. This can come in the form of prayer, meditation, or contemplation. However, whichever practice one chooses, there needs to be a suspension and surrendering of the outer circumstances, a direction inward, and a deep listening. Through learning Buddhist meditation, this came in the form of a deep listening in the silence.

In my Christian upbringing, this was a listening to the will of God. For Muslims, this begins with a verse from scripture which creates a suspension of time, then through the prostration and bowing, one is a surrendering to Allah. This physical gesture in Muslim prayer symbolizes the movement from the outward to the inward, a dialogue with the divine. Practicing mindfulness can come in many different forms. However, it requires a discipline and devotion to quieting the outside world of definition and identification and a listening to another source, one beyond space and time.

This first step in cultivating an inner life is also the first step of self-reliance and of your adolescent taking responsibility for their life. Without this practice of mindfulness and inner solitude, the distractions of the world can continue to erroneously define them and create an image of themselves rather than a recognition of their true nature. Going back to Plato's analogy of the cave, their authentic self becomes a mere shadow of who they truly are. This self as shadow creates a feeling of inadequacy, superficiality, and inauthenticity; it negates them as an incarnated being in time and space.

Non-Linear Time

Creating mindfulness puts the adolescent in an authentic relationship with time. It pulls them out of their linear sense of time and provides them an experience of timelessness, of being out of time, and not dependent on it; it allows them to experience their spiritual eternal nature.

Martin Heidegger writes about this in *Being and Time.* He begins by defining ontology as a reason for being. He arrives at the conclusion that the defining of being can only be done by beings, or, rather, by those who are experiencing being-ness. This, he concludes, requires an understanding of our authentic selves as *da sein*, or "being there." *Sein* (being) is the eternal, timeless part of who we are and *da* (there) is the historical, linear part of who we are. These are two existences; eternal and temporal come crashing together and *voila!* You are You; I am I. The you/I is the *da* and the is/are, the being. We are both noun and verb.

In the Hebrew story of Moses and the burning bush, this convergence of eternal and temporal time is presented as *ehyeh asher ehyeh* – "I am that I am." This is the name God gives himself when he instructs Moses to go to the Pharaoh and bring his people out of Egypt. In Hebrew, this verb is not conjugated. It is past/present/future in one. The recognition of this state of continuation separate from linear time is the gift of the practice of mindfulness. When I learned to sit in meditation, I went from experiencing the hour as multiple hours to the hour as a moment. The clock time didn't change; only my inner being had changed.

The Quantum You

Once we begin to understand this sense of timelessness in time, we can also begin to see past, present, and future in a nonlinear way. One of the challenges with understanding leading thinkers such as Abraham Hicks and Dr. Joe Dispenza is that we are stuck in a sense of time that only recognizes cause and effect in linear time. In other words, I must do something now and then, in a future time, I may have the result.

Both Abraham and Dr. Dispenza challenge us to experience the future now in the present moment. That is, they want us to create the circumstance of the effect as a precursor to the cause. We can only begin to do this once we shift our understanding of time from linear to nonlinear. Dr. Dispenza calls this shift becoming the "quantum you," or, rather, directing your attention and focus on the desired outcome as a reality instead as a future event. Abraham Hicks talks about allowing the manifestation of what you desire by removing the focus on the lack of the thing desired.

What does all this philosophical discourse have to do with your adolescent? Everything! Once the adolescent begins to respond to the groundlessness (even though it may be self-created) with mindfulness, their journey to success can begin. For it will be a self-directed journey, one they are responsible for and accountable for. As long as you continue to fill them up from the outside with goals based in punishment and rewards, they will continue to retreat into the distracted world of cause and effect.

Social Media and Image Reality

What is interesting is that this is what social media provides for them: a virtual experience of the possibility of creating your own reality. This reality is a non-reality, true; however, it seems more real and authentic than a reality they have no participation in. On retreats, when we disengage, unplug, and log out of that virtual world, we replace it with an experience of authenticity, an experience of *da-sein*. Then, they can begin to feel truly alive.

Oftentimes, after the retreat, when we return their phones and devices, they don't want them back. Once they experience this authenticity of themselves, they do not want to be reduced to the virtual versions of themselves again. On one of our retreats in Idyllwild, two of the girls wanted to go on a local hike. We allowed them to go and asked that they take their cell phones for an emergency. They responded by saying, "Do we have to?" Another student tried to sneak in his phone on the trip. When we found it and put it away with the others, he was really climbing the walls. He was restless and moody. After about a day, he began to shift and settle into himself. At the end of the trip, when I returned his phone, he said, "I don't want it. Give it to my mom." Once the adolescents have an experience of timelessness and authenticity, the virtual world pales in comparison. Like Plato's tree, once the sun shines on the tree, its shadow is just a poor image.

Another powerful result of mindfulness is the recognition of the power of intention. Adolescents seeing themselves as co-creators in their destiny is not only empowering, but also intimidating. It heightens their responsibility, not only to themselves, but also to the world they are co-creating. Taking up their responsibility in this co-creation is essential to their future success. They can begin to see the power of their intentions and the impact their thoughts and feelings can have in their lives. Once they switch from cause and effect to intention-driven reality, they eradicate blame and suffering. They create their reality; happiness becomes a choice. They no longer look to the outside for validation and circumstances to make them feel or not feel a certain way, but rather they turn inward and choose both how they feel and the reality of their existence.

Love and Suffering

The other gift I learned from Dai'en is to gaze into the eyes of another with love. Love. This is a word I am still getting to know and understand, along with learning how to love by letting go. My adolescence was a time of self-righteousness and judgment. In order to not experience the deep cavity of oblivion inside, I used judgement of others to validate myself. If I could put them in their place, I could begin to feel my place. What I thought was love was actually control.

What I learned from Dai'en was to look into the eyes of another and know that they have experienced suffering. This changed everything for me. I began to connect with others in a more profound way. In some ways, it made us all equal. It wasn't the type of recognition that required me to do anything. It was just a reverence for their experience. This was when I first began to understand love. To love another, even a stranger, is one of the greatest gifts of mindfulness. Recognizing that we all feel this groundlessness, that we are all on a path of discovery, that we all experience pain, that we all are trying to overcome suffering, that we all want to love and be loved – this is what I learned, this is what I know.

> *"Compassion is not a relationship between the healer and the wounded. It's a relationship between equals. Only when we know our own darkness well can we be present with the darkness of others. Compassion becomes real when we recognize our shared humanity."*
> —Pema Chödrön

Mindfulness is the capacity to love, to love ourselves, and therefore love others. Without this capacity, any attempt at success will be empty and devoid of meaning. The adolescent's soul will be restless and counting time, looking always for outside measures of success, recognition, and accolades to inflate their inauthentic ego and personality. Their list of identities will never be long enough; their resumes and transcripts never complete. Instead, we just create our resume with this: I am a being, intending this very moment to love and be loved.

Imagine a world where we could accept this as enough, where we could look into each other's eyes with the gaze of love, without expectation and with confidence in each other's capacity of discovery. Imagine your adolescent living an authentic, self-directed life, where mindfulness creates this existence, and seeking and intention are the driving forces rather than the rewards and punishments set up externally. Imagine this as their success.

Chapter 6:

Empathy – The Authenticity of Relationships

"We have not even to risk the adventure alone,
for the heroes of all time have gone before us. The
labyrinth is thoroughly known; we have only to
follow the thread of the hero path. And where we
had thought to find an abomination, we shall find
a god. And where we had thought to slay another,
we shall slay ourselves. And where we had thought
to travel outward, we shall come to the center of
our own existence. And where we had thought to be
alone, we shall be with all the world."

– Joseph Campbell

One of the essential skills you must develop in adolescence is the ability to form authentic relationships. Through mindfulness, adolescents can connect with their inner selves. Through relationships, they can begin to know another. Watching your adolescent navigate their social life can be both painful and joyous to watch. Their vulnerability in learning to trust and share their lives with others, as well as the deep connections they make, is an integral part of transitioning from childhood to adulthood. In childhood, most of their relationships were chosen for them; adolescence becomes the beginning of navigating both loyalty and betrayal. Helping your adolescent nurture their capacity for empathy provides them a context in which to understand others at their best and at their worst.

There are few times when I am reading a book and a line or a sentence takes my breath away. It's like a sucker punch to the gut from God. One such line is in Column McCann's *Let the Great World Spin*: "The thing about love is that we come alive in bodies that are not our own." This quote expresses the capacity for empathy: to see another as I, or rather to find yourself reflected in another. Empathy is a hot topic in many educational circles in the twenty first century. It was named as the new capacity of millennials and Generation Z, a capacity that extends beyond prior generations' capacity for sympathy. Empathy is different from sympathy in our engagement in the other; that is to say, in sympathy we recognize the suffering of another, and we understand it, but in empathy, we feel the suffering of another – their pain is our pain.

Mirror Neurons

This heightened attention to empathy is furthered by the current research on what neurologists call the "mirror neurons." These are neurons that behave as if we are experiencing pain, even if we are just witnessing it. These mirror neurons have been recognized in primates for twenty-five years. However, recent testing in lab rats revealed that these neurons are developing over the process of evolution. More specifically, it is recognized in humans as the capacity to actually feel pain while witnessing another experience pain.

In working with adolescents, what I found interesting in terms of this research is its correspondence with adolescent brain development. As humans are developing their capacity for empathy, so are adolescents developing their capacity for "frontal lobe" thinking. What does this mean? This has two aspects of importance: their capacity for boundary setting, where they end and another begins, and their capacity for long term decision making with compassion. These boundaries prepare them for success by establishing autonomy and self-reliance. When they are not able to have a sense for this line between them and another, their path to success can often be impeded by trying to please or impress others and gain approval for their path rather than having the courage to chart their course, even if it looks different from others. It is important that your adolescent's motivation come from an inner impulse and not be an expectation from the outside.

Shutting Out and Bleeding Into

The first aspect of empathy I would like to speak about is boundary setting. Your adolescent right now is exploring where do I end and you begin. This vacillation between creating walls between me and others and bleeding into others is very typical for this age. Creating walls or shutting out can sometimes be experienced within the family, such as when your adolescent has a distinct urge to separate from you and other family members. The perpetual slamming the bedroom door is the perfect pictorial archetype of this gesture: "You are out there; I am in here."

There is a desire to create their own life, which, in the mind of your adolescent, will be very different from their parents. They often speak of parenting different from the way they were parented, living in a different location, being a different religion, etc. This desire to separate is healthy, as it is a necessary part of finding their own identity. Oftentimes, in adulthood, they return to the values of their parents, but ideally this is out of an independent choice rather than a blind following. The forced or blind obligatory following will often end up in an existential identity crisis later in life. We all know the dutiful daughter or son who followed in the parent's footsteps or in their unfulfilled dreams out of obligation only to wake up in their forties feeling lost and confused, or as the Talking Heads so poignantly said in the eighties: "This is not my beautiful wife, this is not my beautiful car… my God, how did I get here?" As your adolescent prepares for adulthood, there has to be some resistance to others and some clear boundaries of where they end and another begins.

The opposite of boundary setting then is the bleeding into or disappearing into another. This is very common for your adolescent. It is often found among peers, social groups, and romantic relationships. Our media culture feeds this propensity to disappear into another with phrases like "You complete me," or, "You are my other half."

As teachers chaperoning school dances, we could always spot the ninth graders because they always appeared in packs. When one girl would go to the bathroom, the entire group would go with her. At lunch breaks and passing periods, ninth graders would often physically hang on each other like melting candles. This desire to bleed or melt into another is an attempt to avoid being alone – not just physically alone, but alone with one's thoughts, ideas, and opinions. It also is an attempt to not be seen or noticed. Early adolescents are characterized by this feeling that everyone is looking at you, or the whole world is focused on you. Blending in with a group, doing what everyone else is doing, or acting like and speaking like everyone else is a way to remain obscure.

Both of these gestures of shutting out and bleeding into are the push and pull of building empathy. In true empathy, we do not build walls, nor do we become absorbed into the other. As Colum McCann writes, "We come *alive* in the other." This requires us to remain separate from the other as we go in; to not to fall asleep in the other, but to come alive. Cultivating this capacity for the adolescent to learn to wake up in the recognition of the other is one of the paramount needs of the twenty first century. Now, let's look at some practical ways to cultivate this capacity within the relationships of their life.

Cultivating Empathy

Parent-Child

Let me start by saying that a parent includes any primary caretaker, whether the child is biologically linked to the parent/caregiver or not. When you are in the position of being the primary caretaker, a certain relationship is formed with the child. This parent-child relationship is what your adolescent will respond to in evolving their capacity for empathy. They will often begin to play one parent against the other, or grandparent or another adult against parent, forming a bond with one and building a wall with the other. Sometimes, they will build a wall against both, and even sometimes revert to an almost child-like relationship of dependency with family members as a way of melting into obscurity. Thus, it is often associated with not wanting to enter into adulthood, of not feeling they have the inner resources to stand on their own.

It is important that, during this time, you encourage your adolescent to begin forming healthy boundaries by modeling for them their own capacity to do this. Show them examples in your personal and professional lives where you have the capacity to live into another's experience without losing yourself, the capacity to hear the opinions of others without being swept up in emotions of sympathy or antipathy. Demonstrating your capacity to hold yourself open while still being self-contained is the model that is most healthy for adolescents.

In your relationships with your adolescent, it is imperative that you remain objective in their tumultuous emotions and their dramatic episodes, that you listen with openness and love, but remain level-headed and clear. The adolescent years are like a tempest: all is dark, and the seas are rough. In the storms of adolescence, you are their lighthouse until they make it through the night and find their orientation with the sun of the inner light of their own being.

Student-Teacher/Mentor

Rudolf Steiner describes the relationship between the student and teacher in primary school as loving authority. This type of authority instills in the child trust and confidence that the teacher knows what she is doing and has the necessary knowledge to overcome whatever obstacles might present themselves. For the teacher, this necessitates a deep love for the child so that their wellbeing is placed first and foremost.

As the student matures into adolescence, this relationship changes. An authority figure is not the right model. First of all, the adolescent is entering a developmental stage where authority figures are not to be trusted. As I mentioned before, this is necessary for the adolescent to develop an inner authority, rather than rely on an outer authority. Second of all, adolescents love to "out-logic" the rules and codes any authority figure puts in place. If the dress code requires one-inch-thick tank tops, the student will find a three-fourths inch but argue that added to the one fourth inch bra strap, it's okay; or the essay deadline date can be argued away with time zone arguments. Adolescents love to argue, and they don't like rules; hence, they love to argue the rules.

Therefore, it is imperative that the role of the teacher switch from loving authority to authentic human I. An authentic human I is a human being who can stand in the world. One who is striving, not perfect. One who has their life in command, steering and navigating the seas of life with command and grace. My colleague and fellow retreat co-leader Naqib Shifa is one of the best high school teachers with whom I have ever worked. Along with being an excellent teacher of many subjects, he is a devoted Muslim. Along with teaching the academic components of Islam in history and cultural studies classes, he lives his belief, devotion, and commitment to strive. In his practice, including his five daily prayers, the students are drawn to the way in which he lives his life and how he surrendered to a higher good. This has a tremendous impact on the students, as it offers an example of a reverence for life and a willingness to be devoted and disciplined for a higher purpose.

Peer Relations

Probably the most influential individuals in the adolescent's life are their peers. These are the ones they share most of their time with, sometimes more waking hours than their own family. Depending on the social relations, this can be very strengthening or very difficult. When there is an environment of unnecessary competition and an external rewards and punishment system, this can create an environment of conflict and one-upmanship, or the erroneous idea that in order to be recognized, you must eliminate any viable competition, putting someone down in order to appear larger. This is also the type of environment that creates a culture of bullying and victimizing, which also is an immature and antiquated way of appearing strong when you feel weak.

Positive peer relations during this time are found in environments where differences and diversity are celebrated and appreciated. This is where the strength of small schools and small independent study groups can have an advantage. In class and school settings where the class size is too small for cliques, the students are forced to be with people they might not otherwise choose to be with. They are constantly having to adapt and consider another's point of view. Whereas in larger settings, students often gravitate toward others who are like them, where they can find commonality and a similar point of view. Although this can be comforting for the student, it can also provide a way of hiding. It also can mask the development of one's own opinions and ideas, as is usually the case when the leader of the clique becomes the spokesperson for everyone's ideas. The most impressionable students end up adopting the prevailing opinion of the group.

The Four Loves

As a person who embraces sexual expression, gender fluidity, and unconventional forms of family and partnering, it may surprise many to hear that when it comes to sexual activity in adolescents, I encourage the students to delay as long as possible. Because the adolescents are still developing their frontal lobe portion of their brain, they are primarily making decisions with their limbic and desire body, which can easily confuse the developing identity of the individual. Oftentimes, adolescents confuse sexual activity as a way of "proving" their love for one another. That is not love.

In looking at C.S Lewis' four loves, this is the Venus aspect of love, or *eros*. It can end in superficiality if the other aspects of love have not been developed. For Lewis, *eros* can transform when one desires the individual over the group; that is, when it is a desire for not any woman or man, but rather for a particular woman or man. Because adolescents are still developing a sense of the true individual, this is not completely possible. Even in relationships where there is a desire for a particular girl or boy, it is usually the case that the individual is not recognized as a true individual but rather what they represent. That is why it is important during adolescences to cultivate the other forms of love before the development of *eros*. These other forms of love help strengthen the capacity for empathy.

Love of family and others with whom we share a culture and common understanding, for Lewis, is *storge*. This type of love helps ground adolescents in their culture; not in a smothering type of way, which Lewis warns against, but in a foundational way, a place to rest one's feet, to feel on solid ground and look out into the world.

Lewis names the friendship-type of love *philia*. I am happy to see this type of love making a comeback. For much of my own adolescence, affection, especially between men, was shunned. The newer generations are bringing not only more acceptance with gender fluidity and sexual orientation, but they are also bringing back the acceptance of loving affection among friends. Although this, too, can have its downside, it is a generally a healthier way to develop our capacity to know another on a deeper level. It can separate intimacy from sex and develop fondness and caring.

The fourth, and I would say most important, love to develop in the adolescent is *agape*, or charity. This is the love that takes us out of our own needs and puts us in service to another. This is the highest form of love.

In the Bhagavad-Gita, this is spoken of as the ability to act without attachment to the results of one's actions. I often present the students with the following when I am teaching out of the Bhagavad-Gita: What acts do you do where the results do not have a consequence to you? For example, if we pass by someone on the street who is asking for money and we give him money, are we concerned with how he spends his money? Does it matter if he buys food or drugs? This often gets a great discussion going, a discussion that is cultivating this capacity for empathy, for often what the students discover is the degree to which we are invested in what the man does with the money corresponds to the degree to which we trust his decision making. This type of awareness is the development of empathy.

Empathy requires trust in our own decisions and in the decisions of others. It requires that we recognize when a storm approaches in the life of another, but that we are confident in their ability to navigate that storm and captain their ship. Empathy requires that, when entering into the life of another, we see ourselves come alive.

Chapter 7:
Risk– The Necessary Part of Growth

*"The cave you fear to enter
holds the treasure you seek."*
– Joseph Campbell

nyone who has constructed their home, business, or been involved any type of construction knows that the project always takes twice as long as you think and is twice as expensive – welcome to parenting adolescents. The project is never as easy as it was imagined. There are times you want to tear down and start over, abandon the project all together, second guess your plans, or fire the lead construction foreman and do it yourself. The adolescent brain is often given the phrase "still under construction." This phrase is derived from recent studies using Magnetic Resonating Imaging (MRI) and functional Magnetic Resonating Imaging (fMRI) to track the areas of the brain that are fully developed and areas of the brain still developing as we age.

These images reveal that the adolescent brain primarily is making decisions with the limbic portion of the brain, leading to more impulse-driven decisions. The frontal cortex, which is responsible for impulse control, delayed gratification, and long-term planning and judgment, is still under development and will not reach maturity until sometime in the early twenties. Therefore, the adolescent brain is "still under construction" and more prone to risky behavior and instant gratification without regard to long term consequences. The studies of the adolescent brain are often used to explain risky behavior such as drinking and driving, unprotected sex, substance abuse, etc.

Under Construction, but Flexible

Although the adolescent brain is still under construction, there is a more positive aspect to this as well: it holds the potential for a tremendous amount of growth. Staying with the construction model, the brain "still under construction" has the possibility to change, morph, and grow in areas before the project is complete. Later, any changes, although possible, require a more thorough remodel. In the adult biography retreats and workshops that I lead, I witnessed these later construction projects require tearing down of walls and messy and costly renovations. Our adolescence may be the last time to be sure that the home for the soul will suit it for years to come. There will always be a need for repairs, maintenance, and sometimes renovations, but having adequate space for the soul to develop is essential.

Risk-taking vs. Recklessness

During the construction phase of development, it is important to encourage growth and innovation, but not to the point of destruction. It is true that adolescents engage in risky behavior, but this does not give them a license for recklessness. Risk-taking involves getting out of their comfort zone, challenging their ideas of themselves and their limitations, risking their comfort to serve another in need, putting themselves out there and having confidence in the vulnerability, and knowing that they may try something and fail and that is okay. Risk taking requires both courage and thoughtfulness, whereas recklessness requires neither. This may seem like a surprising statement, as recklessness is often associated with bravado, the ultimate act of courage. However, recklessness does not require courage. It is ego driven.

Courage and Connecting to the Divine

Courage is associated with what we have to lose from our innermost soul. The word is derived from the Old French *corage,* or, "heart." When we have true courage, we are putting our heart on the line. We are offering up our most sacred and precious part of who we are, in order that it may prevail, not that it will be demolished. Whether we are remembering the tremendous acts of courage of Martin Luther King, Rosa Parks, Ghandi, Rukhsana Kausar, or Irena Sendler, they all share the same aspects of courage and risk taking. Regardless of the outcome to their own lives and well-being, their vulnerability offered their heart up to spread love.

This offering surpasses and rises above the outcome. Martin Luther King's assassination did not assassinate his message. Irena Sendler's beating and torture by the Nazis did not take away the 2,500 children's lives she saved. This type of risk-taking and courage is not reckless; it is necessary in the face of evil and injustice. Whether this level of courage will be offered to us in our destiny is a topic of further conversation. It is important to recognize the difference: Risk-taking is courage of the heart, in order that our purpose and cause will prevail regardless of our own well-being, including our life. Recklessness has no altruistic prevailing motive. It is pure impulsiveness without thought to the higher outcome that can endure.

As I mentioned, this level of courage is a matter of destiny. However, the aspect of risk-taking versus recklessness is still at the heart of education for the adolescent. If risk-taking involves the offering up of something precious and vulnerable, how can we encourage this in the adolescent in healthy ways? Encourage art and cultivate artistry in life.

The Artistry of Risk

Becoming an artist of risk does not mean that everyone becomes a painter or sculptor; it means that we become artists of our lives. We take hold of the materials we are given and transform the material into an expression. This requires tremendous risk, and adolescents are the most talented artists when they create with courage. In order to create with courage, adolescents need to feel they are in a safe but challenging environment, a place where they can make mistakes without being defeated, where they can be challenged and pushed beyond their comfort zones, but with the necessary tools to continue the creation.

The best way to cultivate this capacity is through making art. Whether it's unintended paint strokes, collapsing clay models, or playing the wrong chord, art requires us to come up against ourselves. Art engages us in the process of working through, enduring, and persisting past the feeling of failure and inadequacy. Unfortunately, in most educational models, art has become a subject of election and available only to the students who are pursuing an artistic discipline. Art should be part of the education of every human being, not with the goal of creating more trained artists but rather with the goal of developing our capacity to be artists and beings in the process of creating. Through the process of creating, we learn the value of risk-taking.

Risk-taking of Youth

In an age where we equip our children with many safety devices and tracking systems, it may seem odd to encourage risk. However, risk is a necessary stage of development not just from a physical developmental perspective but also from a soul/spiritual perspective. Risk is important to a healthy development of the brain.

In early childhood, the risk of activities like tree climbing and running on asphalt give them opportunities to not only develop their motor skills and sense of balance but also their risk assessment skills that can foster the development of the portion of their brain that responds to risk reward.

When I was younger, my friend decided to ride his skateboard down a very steep hill and have a few of his friends watch (this was before the opportunity to benefit from notoriety by filming and posting the event). The idea that he would risk this just for the thrill of it and the witnessing of a handful of friends seems very risky. He started off quite well, looking balanced and stable – his longer 1970s hair blowing in the wind, his legs bent at a crouch, arms outstretched horizontally. He was the picture of balance, grace, skill, and technique. Then, about halfway down the hill… *speed wobbles!* This occurs when the board is going too fast for the wheels to compensate and respond to the rider's balance corrections. The picture of grace and skill suddenly became erratic and flailing. The board shot up into the air as did my friend, landing on his knees and finishing the ride down the hill skin to asphalt. We all ran over to find his lower legs bare of skin and the many rocks of asphalt embedded into his knees and shins. He survived.

Too risky? Or necessary? What happened as a result of this behavior? First, there was a story to tell, as it is almost forty years later and I am still telling it – so is everyone who was there. The idea that there is a story to tell may seem insignificant; however, story is important. Our stories of risk allow others to live through them. Although we did not experience the fall my friend did, we can imagine both the thrill of the beginning and the suffering of the end. Through our capacity for empathy, we are able to live through his experience. However, this living-through can only happen if we lived through something similar ourselves. We need to have an experience to link the story to in order for it to have the effect.

Malala

Let's look at another story of risk that is more universally known: the story of Malala Yousafzai. In her book, *I am Malala*, Malala Yousafzai recounts the day she and two of her friends were shot by the Taliban for violating the law against girls attending school. They were transported each day in the back of a covered truck. The idea that attending school is a risk to one's life is something hard to imagine for those of us who had the privilege of attending school without risking our lives. However, the story serves as both a reminder of our freedoms and a story of risk.

For Malala, attending school was not a question. She didn't see it as a risk to her life. What she saw as a risk to her life was not attending school or listening to her heart, which gave her the courage to defy the Taliban. Malala is a special person. Few in our lifetime are given this opportunity. However, it is because of her great courage that she offers the story that we may all live through. The remarkable part of her story, however, is not the day of the shooting. It is her survival and response to the shooting. She chose to not have any hatred for the men who shot her and she has no wish for retaliation. She writes, "They thought that the bullets would silence us, but they failed. And out of that silence came thousands of voices. The terrorists thought they would change my aims and stop my ambitions. But nothing changed in my life except this: weakness, fear, and hopelessness died. Strength, power, and courage was born."

Risk and Soul Development

How does risk help with soul/spiritual development? Recalling the anthroposophical understanding of the body, soul, spirit from Chapter 5, we can see how risk is essential to the incarnation of the spirit within the physical body. The soul, as the harmonizing force between the physical and spiritual, finds necessary opportunities for the spiritual to experience the physical in order to find balance and develop. These opportunities sometimes involve meeting boundaries and understanding the laws of physics.

For example, my skateboarding friend was able to meet the physical world and its boundaries in his risky behavior of skateboarding down a hill. He not only encountered the asphalt and found the boundaries of the physical world, but he also encountered the laws of physics and laws of velocity and wheel rotation, friction, etc. In this case, the spiritual aspect of his being came into relationship with the physical world and its laws. Through the harmonizing of the soul, this played out not just in a physical development but also in a soul/spiritual development. This friend later studied finances and became a business owner and a successful executive recruiter, often taking financial risks to achieve success.

There is no doubt that his soul was searching for physical experiences that were preparing him for future needs. Fortunately, he grew up in an age of kids roaming the streets and not being supervised, as I am sure that almost any adult I knew at the time would have stopped this act from happening. It is also important to note that the idea that it was not filmed or could have been driven by some type of notoriety allows the act to have a more profound impact on the soul development. There is something about the story that exists as a legend-like tale and not a post that preserves its potency for the soul development.

In the story of Malala, we can experience the complimentary effect. Her risk was primarily dominated by a soul/spiritual act. The act of going to school each day wasn't particularly physically challenging. She wasn't required to climb an enormous mountain. Her act of courage was a spiritual deed. However, this too became a story that lives on in the lives of others, and the effect of the story is manifested more in a physical way. Malala and her story are responsible for the opening of hundreds of schools where girls can attend safely.

It is interesting that my friend's skateboard risk, as primarily a physical risk, had an impact on his soul/spirit and then spread to other people in a non-physical way, whereas Malala's attending school risk, as primarily a soul/spiritual risk, had an impact on her physical reality. The spirit is constantly searching for physical experience, and therefore through our soul development these two realms of physical and spiritual continue to affect one another.

Risk requiring courage is necessary for our physical/soul/spiritual development. On the retreats, we find opportunities for healthy risk-taking that allow the students to understand the importance of risk, not just recklessness for notoriety or recklessness to harm one's self. My friend's skateboarding incident was not for notoriety nor was he trying to get hurt. He assessed to the best of his ability and then found where his calculations fell short. Malala, as an adolescent, was not risking her physical body primarily (yes, her physical body was in harm's way, but her act was not a physical act) but rather her soul/spiritual body.

The retreats allow the student to find the opportunities in their own lives to have the courage to risk their physical bodies and their soul/spiritual in order to find their destiny, balance, and harmony.

The Courage to Fail

When the adolescent takes risks, they may experience failure. This is important as well. However, failure should not be defeat. Failure is opportunity, a steppingstone across the river of life toward their destiny. They may slip, but they do not need to give up. Defeat is the inability to get up and drowning in the river. This can happen when time becomes stuck and collapsed on itself, and there is no possibility for a different outcome. The present moment collapses into the future.

Failing is the opposite. Here, time also collapses; however, their future intention, their destiny, collapses into the present, allowing them to see the possibility for something different to happen. When this occurs, failure can be one of the best motivators, the best indicators of success. It all depends on how they respond to the failing. Time exists within them, not without. Therefore, they can decide how each moment will inform their own story.

Chapter 8:
Grit – The Value of Resiliency

*"Opportunities to find deeper powers within
ourselves come when life seems most challenging."*
— Joseph Campbell

I f the courage to take risks is one component of soul development, the partner to risk is grit. Grit is the wherewithal to step into the unknown and stay, endure, and have patience. One of the readings that we often share with adolescents on the retreats is Herman Hesse's *Siddhartha*. Hesse tells the story of Siddhartha's encounter with his father when he decides to leave home.

Siddhartha had a life of luxury and ease. He was a Brahmin's son and was in the best station in life one could ask for. And although he did his duty, performed his prayers, and was considered very acute intellectually and spiritually, he felt empty inside. Then, one day, three samanas (wandering ascetics) came through his village. They took up a life of denying themselves any worldly comforts, finding solace instead in deprivation, poverty, and withdrawal from society. They are unbathed, skinny, bleeding, and scabbed. They are avoided by everyone and looked at with disgust. So, it is understandable that when Siddhartha, as an adolescent boy, went to his father to ask permission to join them, his father refused.

What follows this initial ask and refusal is the importance of the story. Siddhartha informed his father of his wish and not only asked for his permission but also said he will wait until his father grants him his permission. His father said no, forbid Siddhartha from asking a second time, and got up to leave. Siddhartha continued to stand unmoved. When his father asked him why he continued to stand there, Siddhartha only replied with, "You know why."

His father left the room, and each time he passed by, he saw his son continue to stand in the same spot. His father tried to go to sleep, but was unable to sleep knowing his son was continuing to stand in silence. Even the next morning, the father came out of his room to see Siddhartha standing in the same spot. His father went to him and said, "You will eventually get tired."

Siddhartha responded, "I will get tired."

"You will die," his father said.

Siddhartha replied, "I will die."

But, as his father saw that although his legs were shaking, his eyes were absolute. He realized that even though Siddhartha's body was still present and obeying his father, his heart already left and joined the semanas. His father granted him permission to go. This attitude and determination is grit. We often choose this as one of the readings on the retreat as a way to begin the conversation about the importance of commitment and following through. We ask the adolescents if there were examples of things in their life for which they would stand through the night. Most of the time, the adolescent couldn't recall having that level of tenacity. This often leads to an intriguing chicken and egg conversation. What comes first: the circumstances that cause one to take a stand, or the grit to take a stand when it would be easier to acquiesce to a life of comfort and ease? Sometimes, our courage gets us to the precipice and opens our heart to the jump, but it is through patience and endurance that we navigate the flight. This takes real grit.

Finding Endurance Outside Our Comfort Zones

I remember sitting in on a student panel with alumni students at a Waldorf school where I was teaching. One of our students, who had a typical Waldorf education free of AP classes and excessive standardized testing, was a very bright and capable young lady with a sharp intellect. She and her parents sought an alternative education to provide her with a more well-rounded experience. Upon high school graduation, she was accepted into a prestigious neuroscience department at one of the top universities.

Three years into her studies, she was invited to be on an alumni panel discussion at an international educational forum. One of the members of the international group asked her how her alternative education distinguished her from her peers at the university. Her answer: endurance. She went on to explain that taking a variety of classes outside her comfort zone, exposing herself to ideas and situations unfamiliar to her, and not being able to self-select out of difficult situations gave her an endurance that provided her with the stamina to see through long nights in the lab and research projects and the patience when working with others. Even though she did not have the formal AP classes, which would have given her more of the academics needed for her studies, she did have grit. This grit combined with her natural intelligence led to her success not only in her undergraduate studies but also in her graduate work later in the same field.

Developing grit in adolescents requires a focused type of thinking; not the dry, academic, AP-preparing thinking that many of us associate with our high school years but rather with a reverent thinking.

Reverent Thinking

Reverent thinking is applying our thinking capacity to seek beyond the sense-perceptible world. In his lecture *The Mission of Reverence*, Rudolf Steiner begins by characterizing *reverence* as a longing for something beyond ourselves or outside of our grasp.

This type of longing is also found in the ending of Goethe's *Faust*. In the story, Gretchen represents innocence and Goethe explores the effect Faust's desire has on her. At the end of her life, Gretchen chooses to face her condemnation and her soul is saved. This act of sacrifice then affords her with the opportunity to intervene on Faust's behalf. It is Gretchen who intervenes for the saving of Faust's soul. She, as the eternal feminine, saves his soul.

This literary allusion refers to the seeking of the unattainable and the desire to merge with the divine, as in mysticism. Our own desire to obtain the unobtainable is this type of reverence. Gretchen's intervention is both necessitated by her ineffability and the cause of it. Faust, as a literary archetype of the human being, represents our constant striving.

Adolescents are also in a state of constant desire, whether this be relationships, sex, drugs, alcohol, attention, recognition, etc. The adolescent longs for communion with the divine, for the mystical, the unattainable. The adolescents I work with (whether they are struggling in school, struggling with addiction, or struggling with the law) all share a commonality: pushing the boundaries of their given world. The pushing is fueled by desire, and therefore the desire is necessary. This is what gives them a relationship with the world beyond their senses.

Our sense perceptions allow us to perceive the external world. We do not need to do anything but simply observe, and our natural powers of thinking are awakened through curiosity. The super-sensible world, however, is quite different. It is not presented to us. Rather, it requires our active thinking to be impelled by the powers of feeling and willing. These powers are necessary for thinking to impel us to seek the spiritual world. Cultivating this capacity for reverence in adolescence can be done in subtle ways; for example, by taking time to notice the miracles of life: the sunrise and sunset, the new growth in the garden, the act of kindness and selflessness of another. These examples display both consistency and endurance, and it is through striving and endurance that we expand our capacity for forgiveness and patience.

Our power of feeling in relation to reverence is in the form of love toward the unknown. Our power of willingness in relation to reverence is devotion toward the unknown. This feeling and willingness, or rather love and devotion, requires courage! They require grit! To stay committed to the striving, even when it seems impossible and unattainable, develops a character of fortitude.

The Danger of Egoism

The danger here is that the ego, or the individual, can lose oneself when one's identity becomes synonymous with the things, people, and activities of the world. In our constant gesture of striving, we must continue toward our goal and yet resist the tendency toward egoism, where the I becomes the world and the things and people of the world are reduced to a role of servitude. A classic example of this is the accumulation of wealth, when things continued to be pursued not for their own sake but rather to support the image of the ego pursuing them.

Leaving Identities Free from Behavior

The adults in an adolescent's life play an important role in guarding against egoism. It is imperative that they refrain from reducing the adolescent to their worst mistake or to their greatest achievement, and instead leave their identity free from their behavior. During this time, adolescents are trying out identities. It is important that they see this trying out as a garment wearing or changing outfits. You can help them with this by continuing to address their highest selves, free from the garment of the day or hour.

This is easy to see in terms of not reducing them to their mistakes. For example, if a student is caught cheating on a test, they are not a cheater, but rather, someone who chose to cheat. This may seem like a play on semantics, but it is more important than one would think.

Ralph Waldo Emerson devotes his essay "Nature" to this important distinction. He challenges us to understand the difference between "a human who farms" and "the farmer." Similarly, the students need to be left free from their actions while becoming who they are. This includes not only reducing the adolescent to their mistakes but also reducing them to their greatest accomplishments. *Yes, you read that right... reducing them to their greatest accomplishments.* I have witnessed this mistake over and over again. Parents and teachers, with the very best of intentions, praising and turning the student's behavior into their identity, so that a student who performs well on an exam becomes a good student, a football player who performs well becomes the star quarterback, etc.

The problem with the reduction of identity is that it reduces them to their performance and overlooks their spiritual composition. Therefore, if the student performs poorly on one test or the football player suffers an injury that prevents his playing, their identity is so enmeshed in that one facet of who they are, that they have an identity crisis.

It is wonderful to praise, and I highly encourage that you do praise their accomplishments and achievements, but you need to leave them as behaviors. "You did excellent on that exam," or, "Your work on that project was amazing," or, "Your performance in that game was great" – use language that does not turn their performance into a noun linked to their identity. Leaving their identity free allows them more mistakes, more opportunities to fail, and more opportunities to grow and develop grit.

Cultivating Clear Thinking is Freedom

Another aspect of grit when it comes to academics is the cultivation of real thinking. In the lecture by Steiner mentioned above, he characterizes the use of the will forces toward the unattainable goal as devotion toward it. It is the endurance and grit to keep going; it is devotion. He continues by saying that when this devotion or will is not accompanied by thinking, "the soul faints."

This soul fainting is caused by the effect that our love toward the unattainable can have if it is not accompanied by clear thinking. Love (feeling) without thinking becomes sentimental enthusiasm. It is like sleep walking through life, when one imagines a perfect reality and finds no need to change or commit to something in order to change their circumstances. When our devotion, will, love, and feelings, are not tempered with thinking, we become followers who need to have truth and knowledge prescribed to them. But when the willing through devotion and the feeling through love lead the thinking through reverence, we arrive at the educated soul – the ego of the individual who lives in freedom.

Overcoming Procrastination

The importance of clear thinking is also associated with commitment and follow through. One of the greatest plagues to human ingenuity and creativity is procrastination and idleness. This human tendency is also the source of frustration for many parents, who feel that with all the resources and gifts the adolescent has, they are wasting their life away in front of a screen or other source of distraction. This predilection of humanity has been discussed for ages and can be traced back to the ancient Greeks, who called this tendency to choose what we do not want, *akrasia,* or "without strength." In Plato's dialogue *Protagora*s, Socrates challenges the notion that anyone would choose anything but the good. He claims that humans naturally want what is the good and therefore will choose it, given the choice. Therefore, he concludes that any decision made that is not the best decision was made out of ignorance or lack of knowledge.

Aristotle, however, saw *akrasia* as a problem with our desire body overriding our rational thinking. He, therefore, labeled the term *enkrateia,* or "power over," as the antidote to override our desire body in order to make a decision that would ultimately have the best outcome.

Where does this power to override out desires come from? For example, if your adolescent says they would like to go to college, and yet continues to make choices that reduce their options, how do you encourage them to change their trajectory? How do they override their desire for idleness and procrastination for the desired ultimate goal? Through endurance and grit. Through the ability to use our thinking to help balance our feeling and engage our willing to decide and act according to our knowledge. This may seem simple, but it is not. It takes development and cultivation. It takes grit.

This cultivation of grit through thinking is not about studying more or learning more. As in the example of desire to go to college above, it is not a lack of knowledge that leads to bad choices. It is not as if the adolescent doesn't know what is required to get into college. The thinking that is needed here is the type of thinking that is associated with frontal lobe thinking: the ability to delay present gratification for a future result or desired outcome. Remember, adolescents do not have this portion of their brain completely developed, which is why they primarily are making decisions with their desire body.

Striving Role Models

While the frontal lobe portion of their brain is continuing to mature, the presence of striving adults in the adolescent's life is important. Please note: *striving adults, not perfect adults.* One of the mistakes I see parents and teachers make over and again is displaying their strengths and masking their weaknesses to appear less vulnerable in front of adolescents. For example, in high school teaching, one of the factors that is often overlooked is that the teacher, in most circumstances, is teaching out of the subject of their strength. For example, a high school math teacher, more than likely, was good at math and pursued that subject because it was their strength. Their ability to understand the struggle that a student may be having is based on theory but not necessarily out of an experience. In an unspoken way, the student has the feeling that the teacher can't really relate to their frustration because it appears that the teacher just naturally gets math.

However, if the teacher can share examples of struggles they had in other subjects or in other challenges in life, the student can begin to see that the path to success comes through commitment and endurance, not just natural ability. This requires the teacher to be more vulnerable. Please do not misunderstand this to mean that adults have license to behave irresponsibly and recklessly in front of adolescents. No, quite the opposite. While their developing frontal lobes are maturing, it is essential that they are around healthy, well-developed egos – that is, adults who have their lives in order and who consistently override their desires with thoughtfulness and consideration. However, when this falls short – as it often will – it is important for the adolescent to see how a human being acknowledges shortcomings, faces consequences, and continues to improve. This constant striving to become better is one of the greatest lessons for the adolescent.

Self-Esteem vs. Confidence

Continuing to witness adults who are worthy of emulation fail, learn, and continue to grow establishes a precedent that they, too, can make mistakes and continue to grow. They will develop confidence. Confidence is the knowing that they can get through something no matter the difficulty. It is not the same as self-esteem. In fact, there are many studies that show that self-esteem does not positively impact education, whereas confidence has a dramatic positive impact.

For many years, self-esteem was encouraged in education. This was the repeated praise and accolades to students regardless of their performance and efforts. The problem with this meritless praise, however, is it left the student feeling like a fraud. However, confidence is very different. Building confidence is the installing of a belief that no matter what the challenge is, whether it be public speaking, writing, math, or sports, they can figure out how to do it. They can apply their will forces and accomplish the task.

Integrity

This type of will-directed education also leads to one of the most important attributes of human development: integrity. You long for your children to grow into adults with integrity, people of their word, and people whom you can trust and rely on, who can admit their shortcomings and failures, who can learn from their mistakes, and who can stay true to their commitments and promises. Integrity is built through witnessing others be truly human and having the confidence to continue striving toward becoming their best selves. In the end, it is also about tremendous self-respect, having enough love for yourself that any challenge and opportunity to improve is met with courage to face the obstacle, endurance to stick with it, and confidence that one's efforts will pay off. It is an entire process that never rests, and this requires grit.

When Siddhartha's father allowed him to go and live with the semanas, it was not because he agreed with his son. However, he told Siddhartha upon leaving, "If you find true happiness, come back and teach me their ways. If you do not, come home and we will pray together and continue our way of life." As it turned out, Siddhartha did not do either. After spending years with the samanas and mastering their ascetic life, he found this life, too, to be empty and vapid. He knew, however, that the return home would not provide anything different.

Therefore, he continued to search for happiness in many different lifestyles. He found success in all of them based on outside measures of success. When he lived with the semanas, he learned mind control, so through making business deals, he became very wealthy, and as a follower of Buddha, he became devoted and selfless. However, he never allowed any of these activities to define who he was;

he never considered himself a semana, a businessman, or a Buddhist. And yet, what he always had was confidence in being able to learn what he needed to learn and endurance to continue seeking until he achieved his goal. He had a grit that came from the continued striving toward what did not come easy but what required constant exposure to discomfort and vulnerability.

Grit for the adolescent is essential not just in education but in life. It is grit that gets them through the most difficult parts of the journey: resolving conflict with another colleague or family member, enduring illnesses, staying faithful to commitments, or losing a loved one. As much as you would like to spare your children from these hardships in life, you cannot. In fact, sheltering them in some ways stunts their growth, both from a brain development perspective and from a soul development perspective. Although you cannot prevent them from experiencing hardship, you can help equip them with the attribute that can serve them: *grit*.

Chapter 9:
Inquiry – The Life-Long Education

"It's important to live life with the experience,
and therefore the knowledge, of its mystery and
of your own mystery."
– Joseph Campbell

Early one morning on one of the retreats, I awoke to find a student who spent the night up watching the fire. I approached gently and asked him if he wanted to be alone or with someone. He just looked up at me and said, "What is it all for?" I knew this wasn't really a question for which he was seeking an answer; it was a statement of discovery. Once the adolescent is awakened to the constant attempt by the world to make them into something that can be defined and categorized, they begin to live with questions that cannot be answered, or rather, they begin to *seek out* questions that cannot be answered. Living with inquiry resists the compulsion to label. I didn't answer his question. I just sat next to the fire with him and together we watched the embers quiet as the sun filled the room with light. I knew that his life was now changed, that he would now direct his life from a place of knowing that all of the answers in the world can never answer the real questions of life.

A recent article by the American Psychology Association claimed that applying self-determination theory (SDT) to educational settings had positive results. This theory (SDT) encourages a culture of inquiry, which fosters internal and autonomous motivation through three essential areas: competence, relatedness, and autonomy. Competence is the experience of mastery in an area of learning. In the last chapter, this idea was linked with confidence as the result of grit and perseverance. Relatedness is the experience of caring for others and feeling that you matter to someone's life. This was mentioned on the chapter about empathy and the building of authentic relationships. Autonomy is the experience of self-directing one's life in harmony with one's perceived mission, destiny, or task in life. In order to do this, one must cultivate an attitude of inquiry to go through life questioning and seeking rather than identifying and categorizing.

This attitude of inquiry also requires that we abandon what we think we know or what was told to us and begin to question, which can lead to an uneasy feeling of uncertainty and groundlessness. In Dave Eeger's book *What is the What,* he recounts the story of Valentino Achak Deng, a Sudanese child refugee who immigrated to the United States under the Lost Boys of Sudan program. One of Deng's earliest memories, and the reference for the book's title, is a story his father told him: "God presented the Chief of the Dinka with a choice: you can have the finest cattle and have dominion over them, or you can have the 'what.' The Dinka, not knowing what the "what" was and tasting the milk from the cow, choose the cattle. The 'what' was given to others."

The Dinka made the practical choice, the one that came with a bit of a guarantee. This "what" that the rest of mankind got represents this endless seeking, the constant search for the "what." It is a search that is never satiated, and its pursuit can lead to both progress and greed.

In cultivating a culture of inquiry, we need to balance the use of questioning between fueling our inner motivation and turning it into a fire of destruction. Goethe's Faust also experiences this in his pursuit of knowledge. Faust, at the end of his life, is desperate to have his endless pursuit of knowledge come to a rest. He makes a deal/wager with Mephistopheles, who represents malevolent forces to thwart human progress. The wager is simple: If Mephistopheles can provide Faust with an experience that is so satisfying that he is fulfilled, he will give over his soul to him in the afterlife. Mephistopheles will be a servant to Faust's desires and wants in this realm, and if satisfied, Faust will serve Mephistopheles in the afterlife. All that Mephistopheles is required to do is provide Faust with a moment so satisfying, he will say to the moment, "Stay."

Later, in a moment of reflection, after his pursuit of complete satisfaction causes the destruction of many lives, he recognizes this tendency in humans to disregard the casualties in our pursuit of satisfaction. He compares it to a small campfire: started with the intension of warming oneself, gets out of control and causes an entire forest fire, and destroys the lives of many.

Adolescents are driven, too, by desire. At times, this desire can get out of hand, and other times even presents itself as refusal to be driven toward anything but staying comfortable. Fostering an attitude of inquiry helps both with internal motivation and with tempering salacity. Through living with questions, they engage their will to pursue or seek after, but the continual question awakens their thinking, inhibiting being swept away in sensationalism.

Deng's experience of encountering other cultures outside of his Dinka village serves to exemplify this insatiable blaze of human greed and want. He began to see why the Dinka chief chose the cattle over the "what." The cattle were known, they were confined, they were enough. However, as Deng also realizes, once you have been given the "what" or been able to ask one question, there is no turning back.

There are many aspects of education that are like the choosing of the cattle. Adopting curricula that is contained, measurable, assessable, and known in many ways may be easier than playing with fire. It may be enticing to parents to be able to log in to their parent portal and have a number represent their child's achievement. However, how will we progress and learn and grow without the "what"? The answer is not to stultify human inquiry and progress, but rather to temper it with our humanity.

Within each human being is the knowledge of what is right. This may seem like a bold statement. However, as Emerson challenges us in *Self-Reliance,* try to keep the law of consciousness for one day before we judge it to be inadequate. Not by following an external rule book or code of behavior, but an internal knowing of what is right for this circumstance, for this person, for this place, for this time.

Rudolf Steiner writes about this moral freedom in his book *Philosophy of Freedom.* It is a common misconception that, depending on individual conscience, would lead to chaos and social anarchy. Steiner writes, "A moral misunderstanding, a clash, is out of the question between people who are morally free. Only one who is morally unfree, who obeys bodily instincts or conventional demands of duty, turns away from a fellow human being if the latter does not obey the same instincts and demands as himself." This trust in the intrinsic goodness of human beings is essential in working with adolescents.

Giving the adolescent the responsibility to discern encourages the growth of their intrinsic morality. However, this also requires that the adolescent has confidence in their inner core. It is natural to doubt oneself. Your adolescent will need to encourage and support; however, in the end, they need to embark on their own journey of self-discovery, self-reliance, and self-direction. You can support this courage to act out of their own freedom by turning over the responsibility to them through their capacity to discern and judge.

For example, one family I was working with was stuck in the perplexing situation where the child refused to go to school. The family dynamic came to a standstill. The parents would issue consequences that seemed to have no effect, and the adolescent continued to distance himself from them and the conversation. When he went on a retreat with us, he gradually began to open up about his struggles.

My colleague and I have the great fortune to have a setting that gives time and space for the adolescents to process their thoughts. Often within a day or two, the adolescent is able to talk about thoughts and feeling that were inarticulate and muddled in the fight between freedom and obligation. You see, the adolescent who presents as ornery and defiant is really struggling with their own need to direct the course for their life and not disappoint the people they love. The adolescent is intrinsically good and wants to do the right thing. When this adolescent finally opened up about his struggles and fears of trying and failing, of disappointing himself and his parents, of not living up the expectations that were imposed by others and even by his own ideas of success, he was able to get to a place of openness.

Once you can get the adolescent to this point, the next gesture is imperative: that is the offering of the question, "What are you going to do about that?" It may seem like a simple question, but it actually is more potent and effective than one would think. It passes the responsibility over to the adolescent, and at the same time relays the trust you have in their ability to direct their life. Having this sense of responsibility helps engage and motivate the adolescent and sets them up for a purposeful direction inter life.

Sauntering and Worthiness

On the retreats with the students, we read and discuss Thoreau's idea of sauntering. This concept comes from his essay *Walking:*

> I have met with but one or two persons in the course of my life who understood the art of Walking, that is, of taking walks – who had a genius, so to speak, for sauntering, which word is beautifully derived "from idle people who roved about the country, in the Middle Ages, and asked charity, under pretense of going a la Sainte Terre, to the Holy Land, till the children exclaimed,

"There goes a Sainte-Terrer," a Saunterer, a Holy-Lander. They who never go to the Holy Land in their walks, as they pretend, are indeed mere idlers and vagabonds; but they who do go there are saunterers in the good sense, such as I mean. Some, however, would derive the word from sans terre, without land or a home, which, therefore, in the good sense, will mean, having no particular home, but equally at home everywhere. For this is the secret of successful sauntering. He who sits still in a house all the time may be the greatest vagrant of all; but the saunterer, in the good sense, is no more vagrant than the meandering river, which is all the while sedulously seeking the shortest course to the sea.

This idea of walking without a destination and leaving all one knows behind is essentially the first step in cultivating an attitude of inquiry. We leave behind any fixed ideas and knowledge and begin to discover the world with new eyes, as if searching for the Holy Land.

The impediment of self-doubt will inevitably creep into the adolescent immediately. They will question their own competence, ability, and skill. They may feel like they were chosen or selected by mistake. In most stories of prophets across cultures and religions, the chosen prophets often question why they were chosen.

In his *Divine Comedy*, Dante also questions this once he learns that the only way out of the darkness is to go through. Before entering the Inferno, he asks the question that lives on the heart of every adolescent: *"Am I worthy?"* This question represents not only our reluctance of taking up the task but also our readiness. For it is only when the ground beneath the adolescent disappears that they can begin their journey. It is then that they can really begin to ask questions, real questions that do not have a fixed answer or can be answered by *Google* or *Siri*.

Embarking on this journey of inquiry, the adolescent begins to not just learn about the world but about themselves. This learning about the world begins to take on further dimensions. As they become more involved in the process of learning, they become more effectual in the answers. In quantum physics, this is referred to as the observer effect – that is, our attention and energy affects the outcome or result. This understanding of education changes everything. It means that the process of learning is a process of discovery and this process of discovery changes our understanding of the world and ourselves. Furthermore, the result of this process is that new discoveries can be made. Certainly, all of the new inventions, discoveries, and ideas did not come about by purely learning someone else's thoughts and ideas but rather by cultivating an attitude of inquiry and questioning, even if that meant questioning forms that support power structures and established systems.

Socratic Dialogue

One of the ways my colleague and I encourage this attitude of inquiry during our retreats is by applying the Socratic method of dialogue. This is a style of discussion that is grounded on a central open question. The key to this question is that it does not have a fixed answer. Even the leader of the discussion must have an openness to the answer to the question. When a leader or teachers knows the answer they are looking for, it distorts the discussion as, unconsciously, the participants are trying to be the one who gets it right.

However, carrying a true question within and posing it to the participants is essential. The goal of the Socratic dialogue is not to answer the question but to begin uncovering the assumptions and judgements we carry with us while exploring the world. For example, let's take the story Deng recounts from his childhood mentioned earlier in this chapter. The open question for Deng and also could be the question for discussion is the title of the book, "What is the What?"

The leader of the discussion begins by contextualizing the question and reminding the participants of the story of Deng's childhood and the place of this episode in the book. Next, the question is asked – "What is the what?" The next step is very important: this is the allowance of silence. Cultivating an attitude of inquiry requires a cultivation of comfort with long silences. This can be especially difficult for today's adolescents, who are constantly stimulated from the outside with all of the distractions available from our devices: Instagram, Snapchat, Facebook, etc.

It is within the silence that they begin to hear their own voice. Until they are silent, they are just selecting out of the noise around them. However, when they are quiet, not just for a moment but for a long period of time, they begin to hear their own voice emerge from the silence. The time for this needs to be longer than a moment because it takes time for the *ethos* of the outside world to subside. At first in the silence, there is a reverberation of what they remember others saying, what they read, what they saw, etc. Once that noise is silenced, there is a deeper silence; then, they have the opportunity to hear themselves.

The next step is the allowance of any thought and the validation of its authenticity and truth. For example, one participant may say, "Not revealing the *what* is just a way to keep people fearful, oppressed, and not asking questions," while another may say, "The *what* is a trick; the Dinka were smart and made the better choice." At the surface, these two offerings may seem in contradiction. The role of the facilitator of the dialogue is not to engage in these two offerings but to follow up with unraveling the presuppositions in the statements.

For example, to the first offering about the non-disclosure of the *what* being a form of oppression, one may ask the question to the larger group, "What is the relationship between fear and oppression?" and, to the second offering about the Dinka making the better choice, "Under what conditions would avoiding trickery be a good choice?" The idea behind this method of discussion is that the discussion continues to reform into inquiry in order to uncover the deeply held assumptions and beliefs we have that color the lens through which we see the world.

In an artistic exercise, this can also be done by asking the participants to engage in a dialogue with an object in nature over a few days. The dialogue follows this pattern: observation of an object – let's say a tree – then going away from the object and trying to recreate a sketch of the object from memory. Then, the next day, taking the sketch with you to the object and comparing what you got right and what you got wrong (this step is only observing, not making corrections to the sketch). Record the gestures of discrepancy and consistency in a journal – that is, what did your memory get right? What did it leave out? What did it change? Then, observing the tree again without the sketch to look at, removing yourself from viewing the tree and adding to the sketch.

Repeat this process over a few days, and what can be revealed through this exercise and journaling are the assumptions the adolescent makes as they encounter the world and how they remember the way they made encounters. For example, some participants may learn that they tend to remember the details, but not the overall picture; or conversely, some may have drawn a rough sketch of a tree, but their memory left out the details. Some were known to improve the tree, adding more uprightness when it was, actually, sagging and decaying; or the opposite, when one dead branch takes on the entire gesture of the tree in one's memory. The point of the exercise is not to get the picture perfect, just as the purpose of the dialogue it is not to find the right answer. The point is to learn how they approach the world, how their questions reveal their positions, and how their memories inform their judgements.

Inquiry in the World

This process helps adolescents learn about themselves by strengthening their ability to live with questions without having to find the answers. It doesn't mean that they don't look for answers to things and take action when they need to. However, understanding themselves through inquiry can help direct them to the answer that they can more likely hear.

Imagine just for a moment if we spread this type of culture of inquiry into larger spheres in life, such as in the workplace, politics, religion, or the justice system. Imagine the next presidential debate set up in a Socratic dialogue, where a discussion about taxes began with, "What is wealth?" Imagine one candidate answers, "Wealth belongs to the individual who worked for that wealth," and another candidate says, "Wealth needs to be shared for the betterment of all." The facilitator posed the questions, "Can wealth lead to a better life?" "Does everyone who has wealth have a better life?" "Does everyone who does not have wealth have a worse life?" "Is wealth measured by profits?" "Can someone actually possess wealth? Can it be measured?" If we were to begin each of the political debates with just a portion dedicated to uncovering our assumptions and dispositions, we might be able to have conversations rather than debates.

Or, imagine that instead of opening arguments in a court case, we began with a Socratic dialogue. As it is now, the questions that are asked in a judicial trial are not open-ended. In fact, the answers are not only anticipated by the person asking the question, but also the questions themselves are used as manipulation tools to make statements under the disguise of a question. The question, "How long have you known the defendant?" is not only a question with a known response, but it is strategically placed to lead the jury down a path that ends in the desired conclusion.

Now, I am certainly not advocating for sitting in a circle when someone is charged with a serious crime and discussing the philosophical and moral dilemmas of things like murder and kidnapping. I am, however, advocating for including an opportunity for inquiry into questions that are not preconceived and manipulated to paint one right answer. Even in the case of American jurisprudence, where there are two sides competing for the jury's buy in, it still does not allow the jury to ask real questions. I wonder what that would be like?

We explore these types of questions with participants of the retreats and encourage them to take their attitudes of inquiry into the world to begin challenging others when they have prejudice and unconscious assumptions, not with confrontation and argument but with inquiry and curiosity. We encourage adolescents to question their own assumptions, make space for silence in their lives, listen to the voice that emerges from within after the noise of the world begins to quiet, and live in the mode of questioning and allowing, observing and self-correcting, and speaking and listening. This approach to learning expands beyond the classroom and beyond their adolescence; it becomes life-long learning.

Chapter 10:
Nature – The Importance of Unplugging and Reconnecting

"The goal of life is to make your heartbeat match the beat of the universe, to match your nature with Nature."
– Joseph Campbell

One of my favorite scenes form Goethe's *Faust* is Charming Landscape. This is when Faust is outside, sitting on a cliff precipice observing a waterfall. He notices that the waterfall is creating a rising mist upon which the sunlight is casting. There, a rainbow appears. However, this rainbow is a bit of chimera; it is dependent on him as an observer. He, then, realizes that this is an image of human striving, that all of our efforts produce a waterfall over life's landscape and then someone, being it human or be it a god, comes by to observe. This act of observation creates the rainbow. The rainbow does not exist without this act of observation. Amazing that Goethe, who was writing this at the end of the eighteenth century, did not have access to the research now available through quantum physics. However, he was able to recognize this very fact: life depends on us and we depend on nature.

Immersion in Nature

One of the essential components in the EMERGING process is the immersion in nature. Retreats offer the participant a chance to "log out," "unplug," and disconnect from the material world of social media and distractions while connecting with a deeper part of themselves. Earlier, I wrote about the need to find one's identity free from outside definitions. This process of logging out is part of this. The world is constantly telling adolescents who they are, who they should be, and how they measure up against others. Logging out allows them to remove those tempting and inauthentic definitions and connect with their inner core, the part of them that knows who they are.

In his essay *Nature*, Ralph Waldo Emerson presents us with a relationship with nature that is unconventional. This becomes part of the foundation of the American transcendentalist movement in the early nineteenth century. Emerson encourages us to immerse ourselves in nature to understand it. He equates the Greek axiom "know thyself" with the axiom "study nature," proposing, therefore, that in order to really know ourselves, we must study nature. He is not suggesting that we get a degree in botany or that we watch the nature channel, but rather leave behind the world of distractions and just be in nature.

> *"To go into solitude, a man needs to retire as much from his chamber as from society. I am not solitary whilst I read and write, though nobody is with me. But if a man would be alone, let him look at the stars."*
> **– Ralph Waldo Emerson**

Forest Bathing

There are numerous studies on the benefits of spending time in nature, including physical, psychological, and spiritual results. In Japan, for example, a study was done with "Shinrin-yoku," or forest bathing. This is a practice in Japan of immersing oneself in a forest.

The study divided the group in two. On the first day, one group went for a walk in the forest for a few hours, while the second group spent equal time walking through the city. The next day, the two groups switched – those who walked in the forest now walked in the city, and those who walked in the city now walked in the forest. After each walking session, the participants were tested for cortisol levels, a hormone associated with stress levels, pulse rate, and blood pressure. On both days, the participants who spent the hours in the forest had significantly lower cortisol levels, lower pulse rates, and lower blood pressure.

Similarly, in Canada, more than 10,000 people participated in the David Suzuki Foundation 30X30 Challenge. The challenge was to spend thirty minutes in nature every day for thirty days. After the challenge, participants reported a significant increase in their sense of well-being, reduced stress, more positivity and energy, better sleep, and more productivity at work and on life projects.

Another interesting study done at the University of Edinburgh attached an EEG (electroencephalogram), a device to measure brainwaves, to twelve healthy young adults. The volunteers took a one-and-a-half-mile walk through three distinctly different areas of Edinburgh: a shopping district, a park-like green space, and a busy commercial district.

Afterwards, the scientists analyzed the volunteer's brain wave records. The analysis showed evidence of lower engagement of the arousal part of our brain associated with alertness and stress. They also noticed higher levels of meditation-like brain waves when the volunteers were moving into the "green zone," and higher levels of arousal and alertness and lower levels of meditation-like waves when moving out of it. While the volunteers were in the "green zone," they were alert, but it was a type of attention that scientists refer to as involuntary or effortless. This effortless/involuntary attention allows us to reflect, and it refreshes the brain from the hyper-vigilance and arousal that's required in offices and city streets.

Ruth Ann Atchley, a researcher who conducted a study with backpackers, found that spending time in nature increases our creativity. The study revealed that, after about day three, there is a significant rise in the ability to think creatively and imaginatively. She explains that the study revealed that the constant distractions and stresses in life rob us of our forces for creativity. Disengaging for a period of time renews these resources, and we can re-engage in life with a greater ability to problem solve in creative ways.

Obedience

Before we conducted studies on being in nature, writers like Emerson made the same conclusions based on their experience. For him, when a person experiences solitude in nature, the solitude disengages him from society and materialism, because in nature we are immersed with process and the world of becoming. Then, returning to the world, we have fresh eyes and a new understanding:

> So shall we come to look at the world with new eyes. It shall answer the endless inquiry of the intellect, – What is truth? and of the affections, – What is good? by yielding itself passive to the educated Will. Then shall come to pass what my poet said; `Nature is not fixed but fluid. Spirit

alters, moulds, makes it. The immobility or bruteness of nature, is the absence of spirit; to pure spirit, it is fluid, it is volatile, it is obedient.

Obedient? Wait, what? How is nature obedient? Isn't nature supposed to be free? This word obedience seems very strange in a description of nature. Obedience carries the connotation of submissiveness to authority, conformity, and compliance. We often object to this type of outside form. The word can be very problematic, especially when looking at ethical situations when one's conscience is overridden by obedience to an outside authority. This idea of "obedience" seems to contradict the idea of educating "free" individuals. To whom or what is nature obedient? How is this an example for us to follow?

Pinecones

One of the retreats we do each year is in Idyllwild, California, in the San Jacinto Mountains. We stay in a dome house in the middle of a pine grove. The participants unplug from all of their devices (phones, computers, TV, etc.). We spend the morning "sauntering" in search of our "holy lands," and then we move through the day reading, discussing, writing, sharing meals, having quiet alone time, and sitting out in nature.

I have led this trip for several years, and it wasn't until a few years ago that I made the connection with the pines.

The pinecone is associated with the pineal gland, which is responsible for the regulation of our circadian rhythms as a response to light and the production of melatonin. It controls our sleeping and waking and our interaction during sleep with the spiritual world.

Pine trees are also one of the most ancient trees; in fact, they are three times older than any flower or plant species. As they are the most common coniferous tree in the world, mostly in the northern hemisphere, their majesty is shared across borders globally. In addition, each of us has a "pinecone" – the pineal gland derives its name from the pine, as the gland resembles a pine cone, especially its spiral shape (which also depicts the Fibonacci sequence.)

The pinecone is also a symbol throughout legends and myths. The pinecone sits on the top of the staff of Osiris, where two serpents meet together. It is on the top of the staff of the Pope. It is part of the emblem for the Vatican and a sculpture of a giant pinecone "Pigna." In the Hebrew story, it is the place – Peniel – where Jacob wrestles with the angel of God.

> *"For I have seen God face to face-*
> *and my life is preserved. And as he passed over*
> *"Peniel" the sun rose upon him."*
> **– Genesis 32: 30-31**

A few years ago, as I was sitting outside in the pine grove in Idyllwild, I began to make this connection of the pine, the pineal gland, and the spirit. I began to have a new understanding of Emerson's *Nature* essay and what he meant by the "obedience of the spirit." The obedience is not to an outside authority but rather, it is an obedience to one's self and an obedience to our connection with God, or source, or the name you give to this higher being. The pine tree is pure obedience because it knows itself; it knows its task; it knows its destiny. Understanding nature's obedience to spirit, I can understand my obedience as well. For Emerson and the transcendentalists, this obedience is not to an outside authority figure. It isn't even to God, in the religious sense. It is obedience to one's spirit, obedience to one's calling, and obedience to one's self.

One of the exercises we do with retreat participants is writing poems based on our time in nature. During this same trip, I began to notice the pinecones in a different way. At the end of the trip, when the participants were all sharing their poems, one young man shared a poem about a pinecone. He was in twelfth grade, at the time, and in the middle of college applications and waiting for acceptances. This is a very challenging time in an adolescent's life. The college application process can be very material and dehumanizing. It can, if you allow it, reduce the you to a test score and a GPA, overlooking many amazing qualities and genius. It can also be a very scary time for the adolescent, when they are leaving behind a known world of their parents and friends and embarking on another stage of their journey. His poem captures this time perfectly:

Pinecone
- by Ben Ogawa

You have a destiny,
You have a purpose,
But they still may be unknown.
Living in fear and the unknown is frightening,
You can give life and help another grow,
You possess beauty, strength and a great deal of chance,
Such a precious creation you are,
From a distance you may all look the same,
But when explored the true individual shines,
You are dependent on a source
And when ready, you make the fall,
The fall is scary, long and requires great courage,
You will eventually leave your former self
And leave behind memories
And the world a brighter place,
Life, like a pinecone is beautiful.

Nature as Home

On another Idyllwild trip, there was a student who chose to spend his time in nature actually building a "home," or shelter. It was a small tent-sized structure completely made out of the surrounding bits of nature. I watched him over the days construct this very beautiful, simple work of art. However, what was even more profound was the difference I saw in him. He became more relaxed, at peace, and in greater harmony with himself. There was a groundedness to him that I hadn't seen before.

Emerson writes about this ability to create your home, as nature creates a home. Once we learn to be obedient to the spirit, we can begin to build our home, our lives, our futures.

> Every spirit builds itself a house; and beyond its house a world; and beyond its world, a heaven. Know then, that the world exists for you. For you is the phenomenon perfect. What we are, that only can we see. All that Adam had, all that Caesar could, you have and can do. Adam called his house, heaven and earth; Caesar called his house, Rome; you perhaps call yours, a cobbler's trade; a hundred acres of ploughed land; or a scholar's garret. Yet line for line and point for point, your dominion is as great as theirs, though without fine names. Build, therefore, your own world. As fast as you conform your life to the pure idea in your mind, that will unfold its great proportions. A

correspondent revolution in things will attend the influx of the spirit.

Nature as the Ground of Being

I also witnessed adolescents on these retreats reengage in their lives in profoundly different and more creative ways after immersing in nature. One young woman who participated in the Idyllwild trip was deeply spiritual and creative. She became a renown poet and is now an amazing artist and musician. On the Idyllwild trip, she connected with nature in a very deeply spiritual way. When she read her poem to the group, we were all speechless. She managed to connect not just with the process of nature and see her reflection in that process, but she was able to connect with what Paul Tillich calls "the ground of Being;" she connected with God.

The Tree
-by Rose Devika

Darkened clouds cling to the horizon.
The air twisting, lifting, spinning,
Dancing, like a devil's advocate sinning,
My heartstrings ringing,
Reflected in nature's silence,
Beauty,
The only thing louder than violence.

The tree never asks to bend its spine to conform,
Never asks to puzzle piece itself to the social norm,
Stands steady, unwavering, in the face of the storm.
Does not break like thunder, is not pulled under by rain,
Even in destruction it still remains,
Refrains from hostility, needs no humility,
Its durability like that of a tidal wave drifting,
Tectonic plates shifting,
Sifting my conscience to sand.

This hourglass land,
This oblivious concept of human time,
If only like nature we could reach for the divine,
Call ourselves nothing but undefined.

If only we could mimic the way trees do nothing but grow,
Show that if we fall and don't make a sound
We are not battlefields on the ground
Made up of broken bone,
Our very minds and bodies are our home.

When a tree grows it feels no isolation,
Does not become an equation of division,
An algorithm of decay,
Does not try to leave, leave, leave,
It always stays.

Does not ask to trade places with the moon,
Does not worry it will fall like a monsoon,
Tunes its leaves to some cosmic perfection,
Does not ask about our perception,
Needs no map to know its direction.
Finds connection in its roots,
Changes color and sheds,
Does not ask for sleep,
An insomniac in earth's bed.

Our ribs are not cages,
Our lives are not stages,
These moments are not phases.
We are always living,
Learning to be giving like the earth.

Humans in our insanity
Become deities of duality,
Our reality a reflection of the soul in nature's mirror,
Everything becomes clearer when watching the tree,
Existing, twisting, growing, rooted, reaching,
Teaching us to simply
be.

I have no doubt that Rose, like Goethe, is able to perceive something we all connect with, not just scientifically but in our gut. She has a sense that our existence is embedded in the understanding of being, that we exist as both the observer of nature and the object to be observed in nature. The retreat and the opportunity to disengage from all other forms that were telling her what to be allowed her to connect with a deeper part of herself, a part that cannot be measured by quantitative means, such as grades and test scores. It allowed her to recognize her true potential to not just be a contributor to society but to also change society and serve it with her gifts and talents. It allowed her to be, like nature, obedient to her spirit – truly human.

Chapter 11:
Gratitude – The Ultimate Evaluation

"When we quit thinking primarily about ourselves and our own self-preservation, we undergo a truly heroic transformation of consciousness."

– Joseph Campbell

A Glance Backward

I had the privilege of being with two loved ones as they crossed the threshold: my grandfather and my sister. My grandfather had lived a long life; my sister's seemed to be cut short at forty-seven. However, in the final days of both of their lives, their perspective of life, priorities, and time shifted. Life became so precious. It's something I realized we can take for granted. The very fact that we are alive, conscious beings is a miracle that often goes unnoticed.

When faced with death, there is an immediate reshuffling of the deck of priorities.

During the months before his death, Oliver Sacks wrote a series of thought-provoking essays. In them, he shared his thoughts about how he wished to live out his days and about his feelings on dying. They were post-humorously collected in a book titled *Gratitude*. These essays show the same things I experienced with my grandfather and sister. Life looks different when facing death.

One of the most profound differences when faced with death is our experience of time. When I sat with my sister in her final days, time seemed to be suspended. All of the moments we shared together came into the now – the present moment. As we reminisced of days that were in the past, those memories were alive and present right in that room.

In one of Sack's essays called *Sabbath*, he remembers growing up in an orthodox Jewish home and experiencing the observance of the Sabbath. At the end of his life, Sacks brings this memory and experience back into his present moment. "I find my thoughts drifting to the Sabbath, the day of rest, the seventh day of the week, and perhaps the seventh day of one's life as well, when one can feel that one's work is done, and one may, in good conscience, rest."

The meeting of life and death dissolves the linear time of past, present, and future. Being present for the death of a loved one, as well as being present for the birth of our children, allows us to experience time in a different way and value time differently. When confronted with the scope of their lives, both my grandfather and sister, as well as Oliver Sacks in his final essays, regarded their relationships and other intangible things as the most significant, and material possessions as the least significant. Working with adolescents, I come to see their need to incorporate gratitude in their lives. Gratitude allows them to step back from the everyday obligations and superficiality and connect with the things that mean the most to them. This connection instills a sense of belonging and purpose, but in midst of all it, gives them perspective.

Perspective

This perspective of time, life, and priorities is important in the EMERGING process. Gratitude is the final stage because it gives perspective on all the other stages as well one's life.

One of the retreats we do right before Thanksgiving is called the "Gratitude Retreat." During this retreat, we hang chalkboard contact paper all over the room and allow the participants throughout the retreat to write what they are grateful for. We lead them in an exercise, beginning with one's self and gradually spreading out to encompass the world, the cosmos, and beyond. The beauty of the participants being able to recognize the smallest, and yet most significant, aspects of their lives is amazing. When first asked to acknowledge what they are thankful for in life, they have our immediate go-tos: family, health, pets. However, when we take the participants through the following process, something interesting merges. I would like to take you through the process right now. I will describe it, and after reading, you can try it.

Gratitude Exercise

Find a comfortable place to sit. Your eyes can remain open or closed. Begin by just breathing in and out and allowing your thoughts to drift to what is here and now. Notice the temperature, the smells, sounds, and, if your eyes are open, the colors and objects around you. Notice these things by taking a keen interest in them, as if you were just discovering them for the first time. Adopt the curiosity of a researcher or explorer. Continue this until you feel yourself completely present in the here and now.

Next, drift your consciousness to your center. For some, this is their heart or solar plexus, or for others lower in the gut. Imagine a bright warm light emerging from this area, illuminating you from the inside outward, first filling your torso and then extending through your spinal column, then to your head, and then to your lips until you feel the light all the way through the tips of your fingers and toes. Rest in this light. Breathe. Rest. Feel yourself suspended in time and space. Feel yourself exactly where you need to be, surrounded by warmth, light, and love. Bask in this light of love and wellbeing.

Next, share this light as an act of appreciation and gratitude on those things in your own sphere of life. Begin with yourself: shine the light on your physical body, appreciating its miraculous functions, its ability to grow and live, and provide a portal for you to engage in the world — that our eyes allow us to perceive colors, our skin senses warmth and coolness, our fingers and hands can hold and create, etc. Continue to appreciate all of the many things your body can do for you by illuminating this light of love and well-being.

Next, shine the light on the people in your everyday life. This can be your family and friends. It can also be appreciation for the person or people who engineered and built your car, your coffee maker, the plumbing in your house, etc. The idea with this step is that we acknowledge and appreciate all the people who touch our lives every day in seen and unseen ways. Illuminate all of these people, innovations, and work with light and love.

Next, extend to the sphere of your community and political spheres, the ancient Greek idea of polis. Shine this light of well-being and love on the structures and institutions that contribute to your life. This includes local government structures that provide safety, justice, and support: the fire department, the police, the city parks, etc. This includes educational systems and places of learning. This includes places of commerce — having a nearby grocery store that has almost every food accessible. Shine light and love on all of these contributions to your life.

Next, extend the light beyond your immediate neighborhood and community to the geography and climate of your state, including the weather and seasons, the natural native plants, and wildlife. Illuminate this spatial realm of land and climate with light and love.

Next, continue outward, illuminating the entire world. Shine the light on places and people you visited around the globe. Shine the light on places and people you read about from different cultures. Shine the light on people who impacted you throughout history.

Next, continue to extend to through the solar system, through the cosmos, and beyond. Shining light and love and appreciating all of the laws of the universe that enable our planet to continue to live and thrive, supporting life and giving us a home on Earth.

Finally, extend your consciousness to the place of unknowing, to the place beyond our knowledge and comprehension, the far reaches of time and space, where there is nothing left to know but one thing: you are there. Your consciousness and your light and love. Breathe, rest, and illuminate the darkness with your light.

Finish by coming back to where you are. Notice the things around you again, the sounds, the smells, the temperature. Bring your light to a resting place, like the pilot of a furnace or stove. Gradually open your eyes or bring yourself back to your time and place. Breathe. Breathe. Breathe.

This exercise is very powerful. It often evokes tears or gratitude and fills us with an overwhelming sense of love and appreciation for the many small, often unnoticed things in our lives. The example above is a rough outline. Overtime, you can make it your own, highlighting things and people in your life particular to your own biography. The idea is that you start with where you are and ignite your inner light to spread throughout the world and cosmos to a place where you are left with the unknown and your own consciousness. Here you are, a being of light and love with the ultimate prayer on your lips: *"Thanks."*

Treadmill of Success

The cultivation of gratitude becomes an integral process in the life of adolescents, as it helps embed their experiences in a different perspective. Adolescents often magnify their experiences out of proportion. For example, a fight with a friend or a low-test score can seem like the end of the world. It can appear to take on a larger role in one's biography in the moment, whereas time will allow that experience to play a different role. Cultivating gratitude provides adolescents with the ability to appreciate the journey of life.

So much of our culture is focused on the destination, the end result. This paradigm infiltrated our educational system by constantly measuring the students through outcomes and results rather than process.

In 2009, a documentary film *Race to Nowhere* was released. The film is written and directed by Vicki Abeles and Jessica Congdon. Abeles was inspired to make the film after witnessing the pressures of middle school, extra-curricular activities, and the push to succeed made her daughter physically sick. Although she made changes at home, she began to see that the problem was bigger than her own. She saw the push for success infiltrated an entire generation of American youth. As she began to share her experience with others, she began to see the problem as systemic and more consequential than she imagined.

One story featured in the film recounts the circumstances of a local high school girl who committed suicide over perceived academic failure. The film examines our unconscious, treadmill-like choices we make to achieve a goal or reach a destination that is constantly changing and elusive.

We work hard in grade school to get into a good high school. We work hard in high school to get into a good college. We work hard in college to get a good job, to get the next promotion, to get partnership, to obtain the next, the next, the next. The destination that defines success is always the next thing. We never really arrive. The film encourages us to "redefine success for our kids… get off this treadmill together."

The school I was teaching at had a viewing of the film, followed by a question and answer session. The frustration voiced by the parents was heartbreaking. It is as if we all know the harmful effects we are subjecting our kids to in educational institutions, and yet we can't seem to change our direction or course of action. Our society is so invested in the current forms of education it is difficult for any momentum to gather around changing. As parents, you are left feeling helpless and incapacitated to affect change.

Enjoy the Journey

Cultivating gratitude is the first step in stepping off the treadmill. It allows the adolescent to bring their awareness and gratitude to their present circumstances for their own sake and not at the service of a future outcome or destination. They can begin enjoying the process of learning for learning's sake and not to acquire information for a test or a grade. They can begin to appreciate their relationships for what they are and not what they will provide for them. They can begin to accept themselves for who they are, where they are, and not in service to something they are not.

This focus on the present does not negate the importance of goals and achievements. The idea is not that adolescents camp out along the path and refuse to tackle the mountains ahead of them, but rather that they focus on the steps they are taking toward a destination and enjoy the shade of the tree, the wind across their neck, and the smells of the forest. They do not lose sight of the moments they have and do not sacrifice the moment for something they don't have.

This change of perspective also helps the adolescent's identity to emerge from the inside out. There are so many things within their culture that are trying to define them. For the adolescent who is still in the process of understanding their identity, these influences are even more pronounced. Just spend an hour on your adolescent's social media feed to see the many distortions of who they are supposed to be, how success and failure are measured, and how they find their worth in a society that doesn't know its own.

When we lead the retreats for adolescents, one of the first things we do is disconnect from the world of outer definitions. This disconnection, coupled with the reconnection or deeper connection with our inner self, reframes our evaluations of success and failure, identity, and priorities. It shifts the focus from comparisons with others to self-evaluation. Adolescents want to be better, but they want to be better than their prior selves, not better than their peer or the unknown competition applying for the same university. Helping your adolescent evaluate and assess from the inside instills their own inner capacity to evolve.

One helpful exercise to do with adolescents is to have them set intentions and goals and then return frequently to evaluate their progress, make necessary adjustments, and log their growing understanding of their developments. Through this inner valuing process, they find themselves worthy of their lives and worthy of the relationships in their lives. At the end of our life, who we loved is what will matter.

Two Endings, One Moment

Sitting with my grandfather – whom I'll always called Papa – at the end of his life, he wanted me to sing to him the song he always sang to me when I was growing up.

Hush, little baby, don't say a word.
Papa's going to buy you a mocking bird.
And if that mocking bird don't sing,
Papa's going to buy you a diamond ring.
And if that diamond ring is brass,
Papa's going to buy you a looking glass.
And if that looking glass gets broke,
Papa's going to buy you a billy goat.
And if that billy goat don't pull,
Papa's going to you a cart and bull.
And if that cart and bull turn over,
Papa's going to buy a dog called Rover.
And if that dog called Rover don't bark,
Papa's going to buy you a horse and cart.
And if that horse and cart turn round,
You'll still be the sweetest little babe in town.

As I sat by his bedside, holding his hand and singing this song over and over, I began to realize the profundity of the simple nursery rhyme. All of our efforts to provide for each other's happiness, all of our attempts at satisfying each other with material things, are ephemeral and fleeting. In the end, what we have is ourselves and someone we love to sing us a lullaby.

As I mentioned, sitting with my sister during her passing was more difficult as I had to overcome the feeling of unfairness that her life was being cut short and was ending in a lot of physical pain and suffering. It was difficult for my entire family, but probably the most for my mother. Having to watch your child suffer and being incapacitated to do anything about it is a pain only those who lived through it can imagine. During my sister's last night, everyone left the room to get some rest. I stayed with her. She was unconscious. The room was dark and quiet, the stillness of the night blanketed the room. I held her hand and laid my head next to her. There was no singing, just quiet. And then, this overwhelming warmth began to surround me, and I just knew.

The rest of my family came in and, in a few moments, she passed. The feeling that came over me was one of pure gratitude and love: gratitude for every moment of our sisterhood, every moment of our silly shenanigans, every moment of our co-parenting our kids together, every moment of side looks and secret rolling of our eyes at the behavior of others. And, love – love for all of it, not just the good memories but also for our struggles with each other, love for our understanding and our misunderstandings, love for our successes and our failures. That is what gratitude and love can do – collapse time and space into a moment where all of it, every bit of it, is necessary and good.

Oliver Sacks in reflection at the end of his own life summed it up as follows. "My predominant feeling is one of gratitude. I have loved and been loved. I have been given much and I have given something in return. Above all, I have been a sentient being, a thinking animal, on this beautiful planet, and that in itself has been an enormous privilege and adventure."

Chapter 12:
The EMERGING Future

"Follow your bliss and the universe will open doors
where there were only walls."
– Joseph Campbell

When you embarked on this parenting journey, it was hard to imagine what adventures would await you. The EMERGING process is a partner and guide through one of the most challenging parts of the journey: How will I set my adolescent up for a successful and happy future?

Education

The first part of this journey is to reframe the question, "What is success and what is education?" Sometimes, when you reach the destination you were planning and hoping for, it is different than anything you imagined. This is not only true of parenting but also true of our ideas of success and of an education that leads to success. As Tennessee Williams found after his overnight catapult to success, sometimes the green couch is just unbearable, and the room service just makes us fat. For some, being put up in a Manhattan hotel with luxurious furnishings and gourmet delivered food may be a dream come true. For others, this may be what they thought was the dream come true, but it came at a cost not imagined before.

This is also true with success and education. Some may find themselves at an Ivy League college of their dreams and be completely happy. But according to the studies, over half of the those admitted into the college of their dreams are disillusioned. Just as Williams stared at the green satin sofa of his Manhattan suite, thinking his disgust was an indication of something wrong with him, when traditional forms of education and definitions of success do not meet your child, you tend to think there is something wrong with you or with them. But maybe it's just the couch. Once you are able to broaden your understanding of these two paramount parts of the journey, education and success, you can begin to explore many more possibilities. Using the anthroposophical view of the human being helps you understand your adolescent as truly human, connected to the spiritual world, and connected to their destiny and purpose in life.

Mindfulness

By reframing your understanding of education and success for your adolescent, you can encourage them to turn inward and to become mindful. This may be uncomfortable for them at first. As I shared from my experience with Dai'en Benage, the moments of first becoming quiet can become the loudest with their inner restlessness and discomfort with the silence. This mindfulness is one of the essential components of the retreats – once the participants quiet their inner need for distractions, the journey toward mindfulness, inner peace and tranquility can begin. This journey inward also has the benefits of collapsing time. They will begin to experience the artificial and contrived sense of linear time, that cause and effect are not assigned to linear time but rather to free will and the decision to act in any moment and thereby bring the future to the now. This supports your new understanding of education and success, because the adolescent no longer experiences their desire as something they are working toward but rather something they choose in this moment, right here, right now.

Empathy

Cultivating mindfulness allows the adolescent to connect authentically not only with themselves and their destiny but also with others. Forming authentic relationships is an important part of the EMERGING process and the journey. On the retreats, we explore the different ways adolescents can both express their love and understanding of one another and keep their individuality intact. Empathy was named as one of the new capacities of the upcoming generations.

It is important to understand the difference between sympathy and empathy, especially the diminishing factor of one staying awake in empathy rather than falling asleep or merging with as in sympathy. This staying awake when acting out of compassion requires clear boundaries. Seeing the different forms of relationships – parent/child, student/ teacher, peer/peer – in light of the different forms of love that can help you understand how empathy fosters the type of collaboration where each contributes out of their gifts and learns from others. Through this exchange, they can reach their goals together and support of each other as individuals.

Risk

Once the adolescents put themselves in authentic relationship with one another, they become more vulnerable to challenges that will support their growth. Living an authentic life requires courage; it requires risk. The EMERGING process supports risk rather than recklessness. Leading research in adolescent brain development supports the necessary developmental milestones of adolescents taking risks. From a soul/spiritual point of view, this risk also connects them with their higher purpose and destiny in life. Whether the risk involves a teenage stunt like riding one's skateboard down a steep asphalt hill or Malala's courage to secretly attend school at the risk of her life, risk lifts the adolescent out of the mundanity of life and connects them with something worth living for.

Grit

The partner to risk in the EMERGING process is grit. Grit is endurance; it is the ability of the adolescent to follow through with their commitments. This type of resolve requires an inner strength that cannot be forced from the outside. As with the story of Siddhartha, connecting their desires with our spiritual destinies and paths is what gives them the determination to stand in patience through the long, dark night of doubt and disapproval. In adolescents, this can be characterized in the archetype in literature of a longing for a divine presence. Rudolf Steiner's assessment that this longing for reverence requires both thinking and feeling, compelling us through our willing, helps us understand how to encourage grit in the adolescent.

Thinking is a curiosity in the world of the unknown, as Siddhartha was curious about the life of the aesthetics. The feeling is a love toward the object of desire. Siddhartha had a love for wanting to experience true wisdom and peace. The willing comes in the form of devotion or commitment to the goal. Once you connect these three elements of thinking, feeling, and willing toward a spiritual goal, you can understand grit. Out of all of the parts of the EMERGING process, I would say this one requires the most discipline of the adults in the adolescent's life. It requires you to keep your assessments and evaluation of the adolescent's behavior separate from their identity. It also requires you to model your humanness by being vulnerable and fallible but honest and striving.

Inquiry

Current research in education indicates that life-long learning comes about when the question takes priority over the answer. We live in a time where the answer to most of our academic questions can be searched on Google or asked to Siri. Developing an attitude of inquiry, where the answers are not found on Google but rather through experience and human connection, is imperative in the EMERGING process. By beginning the day on the retreats with "sauntering" and approaching the world with inquiry and fascination, we set up the day's discussions to hold a space for silence and contemplation within the conversation. Also, using Socratic dialogue supports the inquiry required to go deeper than just superficial learning and adopt a love of life-long learning.

The artistic activities on the retreats also help to facilitate the adolescent having a deeper knowing about themselves and how their engagement with the world brings about change.

Nature

"Nature always wears the colors of the spirit. Adopt the pace of nature: her secret is patience." This quote by Emerson captures his idea of nature being a model for all of us to learn from. During the retreats, the participants spend many hours with no other assignment than just to be, to be in nature, to be as nature. Nature is a perfect example of the obedience to spirit – that is, to listen, to act, and to wait. In other words, to become your true potential through recognition of one's calling and then the obedience and self-discipline to follow through. This recognition and discipline must come from inside the individual.

It is not something that can be proscribed or forced. A true individual emerges from the inward out and is not a conformity to an outer mold or a fulfillment of outside expectations. One of the essential elements on the retreats is the unplugging or logging out of the virtual worlds. The EMERGING process requires that the adolescent disengage for periods of time from any outside defining, approving, or disapproving force or entity. Along with the research that supports the health benefits of spending time in nature. The poems I shared from the two students also exemplify the soul/spiritual health of spending time in nature.

Gratitude

Gratitude is the gesture we use to close each of the retreats. As at the end of one's life, reflection is both natural and necessary. Each time we go through a stage of transformation, it is important to look back with the perspective of gratitude. This gesture of looking back allows us to begin where we started. With my grandfather, this came in the form of me singing him the lullaby he sang to me; with my sister, it was our shared memories flooding the room in her last moments; with Oliver Sacks, it was his recognition that the Sabbath, the day of rest, comes not just each week but each lifetime.

On the retreats, we have the opportunity to turn our intentions into a commitment to action. In the EMERGING process, it takes us back to the collapsing of space/time reality; it brings the future, here; it brings your goals for education and your aspirations for success to this present moment, where you and your adolescent can take action now.

Follow Your Bliss into the Unknown

We are emerging into an unknown future. The results of the advancement of technology and human capabilities is yet to be determined. However, as parents, you have an inner sense that the current education models are not serving your children. You need an education infused with humanity, with love. These retreats use the EMERGING process to take the adolescent on a hero's journey: departure from the everyday distractions of life; an initiation of mindfulness, courage, and love; and a return to their life filled with gratitude, reverence, and a sense of purpose. It connects them with a deeper, more profound reality. Returning transformed, they are prepared to transform the world. This feeling of being able to transform the world infuses a life with purpose and meaning to follow their bliss into the unknown.

Chapter 13:
The Greatest Gift We Can Give Our Children

"People say that what we're all seeking is a meaning for life. I don't think that's what we're really seeking. I think what we're seeking is an experience of being alive, so that our life experiences on the purely physical plane will have resonance within our own innermost being and reality, so that we actually feel the rapture of being alive. That's what it's all finally about."

– Joseph Campbell

The traditional forms of education are not serving the children of the new generations. Adolescents are sensing this and asking for something more than just information acquisition that is spoon-fed, memorized, and spit back out. They want to evolve their full human capacities. They are asking for more. Even in the realm of texting, this generation continues to search for ways to connect and be irreplaceable. Most educational models are built on statistics and not on the individual human being. We can do better by them. However, you may have realized you can't do it for them. You want them to cultivate inner capacities to navigate life, to go on their hero's journey, to connect with their destiny, and have you there as guides and advisors.

The greatest advocacy and gift you can give to your children is time. Give them back their time and allow them the opportunities to connect with themselves and others in deeper, more meaningful relationships. How do you do this? By giving them opportunities to discover more of their humans through the EMERGING process: *E*ducation, *M*indfulness, *E*mpathy, *R*isk, *G*rit, *I*nquiry, *N*ature and *G*ratitude. Through this eight-part journey, the adolescent will begin to EMERGE into their destiny and be ready to take on the world.

Providing these opportunities can be overwhelming while trying to balance the demands of an already packed schedule. That is why it is important to go through this journey while on retreat. It is important to focus on these steps without the distractions of academic and social demands. The retreats give them the time to just breathe, reevaluate, reprioritize, and transcend time.

Adolescence is a time where a window of opportunity opens to connect with their destiny. From a brain development point of view, the synapses that are wired during this time are crucial to their future. Synaptic plasticity and the release of neurotransmitters are influenced by the environment of the adolescent and wire their brains for the life's journey. From a soul/spiritual point of view, this is the time when they connect with their spiritual reality and begin to see themselves beyond their physical form. Provide your adolescent with the opportunities to take a pause from the business of life and become who they intended to be.

A few years ago, I composed a poem for a graduating class and spoke it at their commencement. It was my wish for them to stay present in the moment and not be swept away from the demands of society constantly trying to mold them into conformity. I would like to end by sharing it with you.

May you have the courage to take on this journey of parenthood and believe in the future!

This Moment

Now in the quiet hush
Now in the perceptible pause
Now in the sacred trust

Remember this moment

When the earth was spinning

The sun was shining
Saturn's rings ringing
The musical spheres singing

And you,
Here
In time

Crossing the finish line
Entering the starting gate
Past and future collide-
Wait....

Remember this moment
Suspended- then gone too soon
Like the silver lined grail moon
Cradled on the horizon
Sliver, elegant crescent rune
Turned away from the plunging abyss
To embrace its own darkness

Remember this moment

Captured from the elusive chase
Like the bathing sunlight on your childhood face
Its meaning hidden in youthful innocence
Its gift realized only in its absence

Remember this moment

When the world is too much
And everything you seem to touch
Becomes overbearing, demanding
Judgmental, reprimanding

When the world is too small
Reduced to a shopping mall
Even truth is for sale
The latest acquisition becomes the Holy Grail

Remember this moment

When you are passed by - not seen
When you find yourself on your knees
Begging for one more chance
Averting the glance...
   of disappointment
      of broken trust
         of utter disgust

Remember this moment

When you are praised for your deeds
When you finally succeed
And all of your accomplishments accumulate

Like a Dantean leaden robe of fate
Its gilded mantle taking its toll
Becoming an unbearable burden for your soul

Remember this moment

When you are lost
When the darkness envelops your inner trust
And your confident solitude
*   becomes abandonment...*

Where are you?
Who am I?
Is this my life?

Remember this moment
Remember this moment
Remember this moment

For, here, on this day
You are loved
Let that lead the way

Don't be fooled by what they say:
"Love conquers all"
Love conquers nothing!
No,

Love sets us free.

Free from the bondage of false identity
Free from the platitudes of charitable pity
Free from self-righteousness
Free from conformity
Free from cowering beneath the world's enormity.

Remember this moment
Love, and in freedom choose
Transform the world
We believe in you.

Acknowledgments

If life has taught me anything, it is this: In the end, there is only love. I have a life blessed with many people who taught me the limitless possibilities when you just return to this simple truth: love and be loved. With love comes gratitude, so I would like to take a pause and acknowledge the people who made this book possible.

My current and former students and their parents, who trusted me to help them navigate their adventurous paths in life. Each of you are not just a student but also a teacher, and I continue to learn from you each day.

Three colleagues, who are my touch stones in life: Jenell Carlson, who was my children's first teacher and became my life-long friend; Bob Dell'Oliver, who was my first colleague and taught me to be fully present with the students by "shutting the door of your classroom and leaving everything else out;" Naqib Shifa, who leads the retreats with me and never fails to connect with me in real heart-to-heart, spiritual conversation.

Dorit Winter, my life mentor, who guided me on the path of anthroposophy by challenging me to be clear in my thinking, honest in my actions, and humble in my accomplishments.

The Waldorf community around the world – may you continue to swim upstream with courage and guidance from the spiritual world.

Pendle Hill – may you continue to offer an oasis for people who need to quiet the noise of the world and begin to listen to their inner voice.

To The Author Incubator team: Angela Lauria, CEO & Founder of The Author Incubator for believing in me and my message and showing me that love can rule the publishing and business world. To my developmental editor, Ora North, and managing editor, Emily Tuttle: Thanks for encouraging me and holding me to my deadlines! Many more thanks to everyone else at TAI, but especially Cheyenne Giesecke, Ramses Rodriguez and Amari Ice for always being honest and compassionate.

Thank you to David Hancock and the Morgan James Publishing team for helping me bring this book to print.

And finally, to my core: my family. My parents, who weathered their parenting adventure with me by continuing to love me without conditions, who provided unwavering consistency and boundaries and always supported my individuality. My sister, Lisa, who dedicates her life to her students and infuses public education with vitality and ingenuity. My sister, Jen, who remains my best friend and is with me every day as my guardian angel. And my two amazing daughters, Maya and Sage, who inspire me each day with their tenacity to live in authenticity.

Thanks for Reading

Thank you so much for reading *Motivating Adolescents!* If you've made it this far, I know one of two things about you: First, you're more ready than ever to motivate your adolescent and set them up for success. Or, you just flipped to the back of the book to see the end. Either way, I am here to support you.

I would love to learn more about your parenting journey and your questions and thoughts about motivating your adolescent. Please keep in touch. I'm most active on Facebook as Robin Theiss https://www.facebook.com/ profile.php? id=100008384677967 and Instagram https:// www.instagram.com/robinrtheiss.

For more information about my work, please visit robintheiss.com for more resources, including retreat opportunities for both adolescents and adults.

About the Author

Robin Theiss is the founder of EVE-Emerging Ventures in Education, leading workshops and retreats for adolescents and adults. She is passionate about breaking down the walls of education and listening to the wisdom of our youth. Robin mentors and teaches students one-on-one as well as adults in supporting their parenting adventure. She travels the globe throughout Europe, Asia, and America, speaking at international teaching conferences and serving on the faculty of Waldorf teacher training programs in China, Germany, Hungary, Taiwan, and California.

Robin has been in Waldorf education for twenty years, working in early childhood, grades, and high school. She received her B.A. in philosophy and religious studies from the University of California, Riverside. Robin was selected as a student in residence at the Quaker community Pendle Hill in Pennsylvania, where she learned the value of mindfulness and the principles of non-violent communication skills. She then continued as a scholarship recipient at Claremont Graduate School to study in the Master of Arts program in the School of Theology.

Before becoming a teacher, Robin owned and operated Natale Coffee. This local coffee house became an oasis in Orange County, offering poetry evenings, open music nights, open political discussions, and book clubs. Through working with her employees, Robin discovered her passion for the youth transitioning into adulthood and finding their way in life. With this passion, she later became involved in the Orange County C.A.S.A. (Court Appointed Special Advocate) program, mentoring foster youth in their transition into adulthood.

Robin has two adult daughters, Maya and Sage, who inspire her every day. When Robin is not traveling, she retreats to her beach cottage in Huntington Beach, California.

Printed in the USA
CPSIA information can be obtained
at www.ICGtesting.com
JSHW080147120524
62938JS00009B/705

9 781631 950346